Exploring
Death
Valley

Exploring
DEATH
VALLEY

Second Edition

by RUTH KIRK

**Photographs by
RUTH and LOUIS KIRK**

**Stanford University Press
Stanford, California**

Stanford University Press, Stanford, California
© 1956, 1965 by the Board of Trustees of the
Leland Stanford Junior University
Maps by Dee Molenaar
Printed in the United States of America
ISBN 0-8047-0481-3
Original edition 1956
Second edition 1965
Fourth printing, with revisions, 1969
Sixth printing 1973

Preface

Death Valley was our home for three years, while my husband served there as ranger. When I think back to those years I find a kaleidoscope of impressions, for Death Valley is a land of contrasts and paradoxes.

It is harsh and unfavored seen in the relentless glare of midday: dry, stony, empty, its mountains abrupt walls, its plants too widespaced to soften the land or clothe it. It is the lowest point in the western hemisphere, the hottest desert in the world, and the least-rained-upon land in the United States. In summer its heat can be so overpowering that simply living through the day seems accomplishment enough, and the isolation is so complete that dust devils and pack rats can seem welcome companions.

But these things are not necessarily undesirable. Desert is land stripped to the essentials, freed of superficialities; and living in it can revitalize one's perspective. Furthermore, Death Valley is more than unremitting, unbroken bleakness. Look beneath the hostile veneer: it is also ducks paddling and quacking in freshwater ponds, wind whispering through reeds, watercress choking a creek, snow capping each peak with a white beret.

This book is intended as guide to both the harshness and the beauty.

Much of the material presented here was gathered during the time we lived in the Valley. Much more, however, is based on the experience and knowledge of others, too numerous to mention here, and whatever strength these pages may hold is due largely to their efforts. My job has been to observe, record, and compile—and to love this valley in spite of its desolation, or perhaps because of it.

RUTH KIRK

Contents

MATRIARCH

The Human Story

To its Indians, Death Valley has been simply "home" for untold centuries. It sums up all that is desert: the sparse, the hot, and the dry. But these were expected qualities, and Indians found no particular harshness here that they had not known in adjoining valleys. It remained for the careless and the romantic among white men to give the valley its connotation of death.

Ancient Times: The first-comers found a climate that was gentle compared to today's, for Ice Age glaciers were still retreating from the land to the north, and the lakes that once flooded much of the Southwestern desert were still relinquishing the land. Probably these Indians merely camped in Death Valley to kill and dress game, for from this period, about nine thousand to five thousand years ago, archeologists find only crude arrow and spear points, scrapers, and choppers. These most ancient men are called Lake Mohave People. Their artifacts lie on gravel benches above the floor of the central valley.

Next came the Mesquite Flat People, who were here from about five thousand to two thousand years ago. They lived in the low dunes of the valley's north end, where clumps of mesquite trees assured seeds for food plus ready-made firewood and wind protection. Hundreds of separate homesites have been found, some with the circles of stones and ancient ashes of family fireplaces still in place. Arrowheads, choppers, hammers, and seed-grinding stones lie scattered about, covered and uncovered by the shifting of the sand.

The third group who arrived about two thousand years ago, are called the Saratoga People. Unlike their predecessors, these people contended with a land that had become harsh. Gone were the soft rains and grass and big game that eased life for the Lake Mohave People and even for the Mesquite Flat People. In their stead were increasing dryness, heat, and desolation.

But man is infinitely adaptable. Saratoga Man learned to fashion slender spearpoints and arrowheads suited to small game. He learned dependence on wild seeds and grew adept in gathering, grinding, and storing. He knew also restlessness and an urge to fulfill more than mere body needs. Archeologists have found not only stone projectiles and grinders but also sea-snail shells, which were traded across long, footsore miles to be strung as necklaces.

The Desert Shoshone: About one thousand years ago, bands of Shoshone Indians drifted down from the north, pushing from their homeland into Piute territory and ultimately into Death Valley. They produced the last of the pre-white cultures. Fragments of baskets and pottery, occasional beads and toys, countless arrowheads and spearpoints tell of their arrival. So do Death Valley's "Indian maps" and petroglyphs.

The "maps" are rocks laid out in mysterious twenty- and thirty-foot rows on the gravel of Mesquite Flat, Emigrant Wash, and the Cottonwood Fan. No one yet has deciphered their meaning. Early-day prospectors sometimes mistook them for representations of trails and waterholes, and got lost trying to make sense of them. The present Indians know nothing about them.

To their makers they presumably had "ceremonial significance," that great catch-all into which twentieth-century man pitches what he fails to understand of preceding cultures. Without question prodigious work went into shaping the maps—finding stones of the right size and aligning them according to plan. And without question they are very old, for they gleam with the desert varnish that comes only after centuries of sunshine have acted on the manganese in rock.

Death Valley's petroglyphs also are old and of unknown meaning. Emigrant Canyon, Cottonwood, Marble, Titus, Echo—the patina of many canyon walls is broken by figures of men, mountain sheep, and lizards, and by circles, crosshatches, and wavy lines.

PETROGLYPHS

BASKET-MAKER

What do they mean? What prompted men to peck out these bulletin boards, or art galleries? Perhaps they record events, or illustrate stories, or point to water, or belong to forgotten rituals. Such are the theories. No one knows.

The early Shoshone evidently drifted into Death Valley a band at a time. Scattered in family groups and forced to work long and hard merely to stay alive, they had little time to develop an elaborate culture. Even so, the seemingly universal human sense of beauty did find expression in the fine basketry of the women, which ranks with the world's best.

Rabbits, bighorn sheep, rodents, lizards, and an occasional deer furnished meat for the Shoshones. They ate green plants and the seeds of cactus, grass, chia, ephedra, and many other plants. Most of all, they relied on pine nuts and mesquite beans as mainstays for their larders.

Mesquite ripened in June and July. Women pounded green pods in wooden mortars to get juice for a fermented drink; and they shelled dry beans by rubbing them between metate and mano stones, then grinding them with mortar and pestle. A particularly prized mesquite food was candy made by winnowing a sticky white powder from crushed beans and pods, moistening it with water, and baking it in round balls in the summer sunshine.

Pine nuts ripened in early fall. Men knocked cones from the trees with long poles and women and children gathered them in baskets, then heated them over coals until they popped open and released their oily nuts. Parched and ground and mixed with water, the nuts made a mush that was served with meat.

Indians Today: Five or six Indian families still winter in Death Valley, which is perhaps a fourth as many as were here before the coming of white men. From September until May they live in adobe houses south of Furnace Creek Ranch (although as late as 1952 one family lived by preference in a brush wickiup tucked among the mesquite near the present Visitor Center). In summer they move to the cooler elevations of Beatty and Shoshone.

Few traditions are observed now. Mesquite beans and pine nuts fall to the ground scarcely noticed; children no longer know the taste of mesquite bean candy. No medicine men remain to minister to the people's ills. The old stories seldom are told. Few Shoshones remember why the gods once flooded the valley and forced the people into the Panamints; or how Bighorn Sheep brought the first pine nuts from a distant land; or that it was Rabbit who shot the Sun from the sky, causing him to fall to earth in Mustard Canyon.

WEAVING A CARRYING BASKET

SHOSHONE
BABY

FORTY-NINERS

Four families from Midwest states and a group of bachelors were the first white people to enter Death Valley. They were on their way to the California gold fields, part of a train of one hundred wagons led by Captain Jefferson Hunt, who had been over the trail three times previously and worked now for a fee of ten dollars per wagon. The party called themselves the Sand Walking Company, a name corrupted from their destination, the San Joaquin Valley.

West of Salt Lake City a pack train overtook them, and its leader, O. K. Smith, pulled from his saddlebag a rough map that he said would cut five hundred miles from the trail ahead. Hunt advised against trying it, but almost a third of the party voted to split off to the west of the regular route. It was a tragic decision.

Historians think the map was a penciled version of a route described to Smith by the Ute Indian chief Walkara, who had recently led a horse-stealing raid into California. Whatever its origin, it was a "shortcut" that added two months of misery. "[It was] always the same," wrote Mrs. J. W. Brier, one of four women in the misguided party: "Hunger and thirst and an awful silence."

Twenty-seven wagons went into the valley. One came out. It belonged to the Wades, a family of five who camped with the other families for a time and then turned south, making their way to San Bernardino without undue hardship except the time loss.

Jayhawkers: Most of the single men who "shortcutted" were banded together as the "Jayhawkers." With them were groups dubbed the "Georgians" and the "Mississippians"—perhaps forty or fifty men in all. For them the days in Death Valley were little different from the other exhausting, often waterless days they had already spent in the desert. A log kept by Sheldon Young, one of the group, notes simply that it was hot the afternoon they trudged down Furnace Creek Wash: it was Christmas Day, 1849.

The Jayhawkers spent only two or three days in Death Valley. They wandered north to Salt Creek, burned their wagons to smoke the meat of their last oxen, and left on foot by Towne's Pass and Jayhawker Canyon.

Traveling with the Jayhawkers, although not really belonging to the group, was the Brier family—a clergyman, his wife, and their sons aged four, seven, and nine years. It was an agonizing crossing for them. "Many times when night came," Mrs. Brier wrote, "my husband would be on ahead looking for water, and I would search on my hands and knees in the starlight for tracks of the oxen.... Poor little Kirk ... would stumble on the salty marsh for a time and then sink down crying 'I can't go any farther!' and then I would carry him."

The Bennetts and Arcanes: Instead of following the Jayhawkers north, seven wagons turned south. At the foot of the Panamint Mountains, probably near Tule Spring, the group made camp. There were two families, the Bennetts and the Arcanes, plus eleven single men. Lost and with little food, they evolved a last, desperate plan: William Lewis Manly and John Rogers, the strongest of the bachelors, would go ahead to scout the way to the settlements that all believed lay just over the mountains.

It was not that easy. The trip to civilization proved infinitely longer and harder than expected. Yet as soon as the two found help at San Francisquito Ranch, near Saugus, they gathered food and began the dread trek back to the stricken party waiting for them in the desert. Ranchers sent two horses and a little one-eyed mule, packed with supplies. A Mexican woman tucked in oranges as a special gift for the children.

Almost four weeks after they had left Death Valley, Manly and Rogers again entered it. They found only the two families waiting. The single men had abandoned hope and struck off on their own. One, Captain Robert Culverwell, had died.

Forlornly, yet hopefully, the families resumed the march west. Shirts sewn together as saddlebags were thrown across the back of an ox, to carry little Martha Bennett and Charlie Arcane. Melissa and George Bennett, slightly older, rode astride. The adults walked.

It was a three-week, two-hundred-fifty-mile trip. The second day, according to Manly's account, they topped the Panamints and turned for a last look at the valley they had feared would be the grave of them all. "Goodbye, Death Valley," murmured one of the women.

DEATH VALLEY FROM THE PANAMINTS

PROSPECTORS

Not many years after they struggled out of Death Valley, some of the '49ers returned to prospect. One of the Jayhawkers had picked up a chunk of silver ore there while looking for a sight that had fallen off his gun. It was only one piece of rock, but it touched off a mining fever that took almost a century to abate, and is not dead even yet.

By 1856 government surveyors had mapped a meridian line north from San Bernardino to Death Valley. On their heels came lone prospectors, state mineralogists for California and Nevada, Boundary Commission investigators, U.S. Army surveyors. One expedition even startled the Indians by appearing on camels! Reports, some official, some personal, soon were announcing that the Amargosa River was navigable, that Death Valley had no plants and was "totally without water," that it was a "ghastly sink," horribly endowed with "sun-dried mummies . . . of whom no trace or recollection is preserved."

The First Strike: The reports were believed, but they did not slow the stampede of prospectors.

The first of many boom towns was Panamint City, high in the mountains west of Death Valley. Men struck silver chloride there in 1873 and a town quickly sprang up complete with more than one thousand citizens, a newspaper, ample saloons, and girls from San Francisco's roaring Barbary Coast.

Brothers from Switzerland started a ranch ten miles over the crest of the mountains, on the Death Valley side, and supplied fresh vegetables and fruits to Panamint City. Wagons hauled in other supplies from Los Angeles, which had recently established itself as the leading city of Southern California. Los Angeles merchants had underbid competitors in Ventura for the trade of Cerro Gordo, a mine northwest of Panamint City, and they welcomed this new business to strengthen their position. They even developed a special port to handle shipment of Panamint City ore to England for smelting. This was Santa Monica, begun specifically to serve Panamint City and to deprive Ventura.

Ore assayed as high as $4,000 a ton, rich enough so that simply displaying it in a Los Angeles bar led to the floating of two million dollars' worth of stock, with Senators John P. Jones and William M. Stewart as the principal backers. Ironically, their loss four years later was to equal the exact amount of this initial stock issue. But, as someone put it, "lots of other millions were handed around between the beginning and the end!"

The ore proved too complex for profitable silver recovery. The bubble burst, the boom town folded, and silence returned to the Panamints.

Borax: With borax the story was different. The *Inyo Independent* reported its discovery in Death Valley in 1873, the same year that Panamint City's strike was made. The price of borax was thirty-five cents per pound, high enough to be tantalizing, but even so nothing much came of the report for eight years.

Then one evening a prospector stopped to visit Aaron and Rosie Winters, a poverty-stricken couple living at Ash Meadows, east of the Funeral Mountains. Their home was a hovel half dug into a hillside with packed earth for a floor and a scrap of dirty canvas for a door. But hospitality is more than externals, and the prospector lingered a while.

He talked of borax, newly discovered in Nevada, and about how to test for it. Sulphuric acid and alcohol poured over true borax and ignited would burn with a green flame, he said.

Next day Aaron told Rosie they were heading for Furnace Creek. He had seen a soft white fluff on the marsh in the sink of the valley and it fit the prospector's description of "cottonball" borax. He gathered samples, powdered them, poured on the chemicals, struck a match—and fairly shouted, "She burns green, Rosie. We're rich!"

The Winters sent a sackful of borax to William T. Coleman, a San Francisco entrepreneur who was backing borax mining in Nevada. Immediately,

BORAX "HAYSTACKS"

TWENTY-MULE TEAM

he bought their interests for $20,000 and laid the beginnings of the Pacific Coast Borax Company. Harmony Borax Works was built a mile north of Furnace Creek Ranch. Indians were hired to cut mesquite wood for the boilers of its crystallizing vats; Chinese were brought in to gather basketfuls of the white fluff that leached from the marsh and haul them on sledges to the refinery.

Through the winter of 1881–82 all went well. But when the thermometer started its summer climb, borax stopped crystalizing on the iron rods suspended in the refining vats. The weather was too hot. Operations were switched to the Amargosa Works, south of Shoshone, where the higher elevation offered lower temperatures. It was there that the twenty-mule team idea was born.

Coleman had hired an eight-mule wagon team to haul borax from the Harmony plant. Now he hired a twelve-mule team that had hauled for Eagle Borax Works, an abortive borax venture in southern Death Valley. This second team handled twice the load of the first, men at the Amargosa noticed. And if twelve mules could pull double the weight of eight, what would happen with all twenty teamed together?

The foreman decided to try it. He ordered special wagons built sixteen feet long, four feet wide, and six feet deep, with rear wheels seven feet in diameter and banded with iron tires an inch thick—enormous wagons sized to fit the promise of the twenty mules. A full rig of two wagons loaded with borax, plus the accompanying 1,200-gallon watertank, weighed thirty-six and a half tons!

From Death Valley to the railhead at Mojave it was 165 miles, a ten-day haul. But wagons and mules served without fail for the five years they were needed, and even today the original wagons stand intact at Furnace Creek Ranch.

Boom Days: By the turn of the century Death Valley had become a mecca for prospectors. The valley's borders were "lined with precious metals," the *Rhyolite Herald* reported in 1908. "Gold, silver, copper, lead, and all manner of metals and minerals are found here. An expert has even declared the presence of diamonds. Salt and borax deposits are the most extensive in the world."

Claims were staked one day and towns developed the next. Rhyolite, perhaps the biggest of the booms, got its start in 1904 when Shorty Harris cut his pick into a chunk of green-speckled gold ore. He named the strike "The Bullfrog," for the color of the ore, and hastened to the nearest bar to boast of it to other prospectors. Men listened, looked at Shorty's specimen, packed their bedrolls, and headed for the Bullfrog. In just over a year a city of 5,000 bloomed where there had been scarcely a white man within fifty miles. Rhyolite was one of Nevada's finest cities. A three-story hotel, a bank, two railway depots, a stock exchange, two churches, and uncounted bars and dance halls lined its streets.

One mine boom merged into the next: Keane Wonder at the base of the Funeral Mountains and Chloride City along the crest; Rhyolite with Bullfrog, South Bullfrog, South Circle, and Brawn City clustered about it as suburbs; Skidoo across Death Valley in the Panamints but linked to Rhyolite by both telephone and stage service; Harrisburg, a tent city near Skidoo begun by the lucky strike of two prospectors who were lost in a fog while en route to Skidoo; Greenwater, Schwaub, Lee. . . .

It was a rollicking era. To celebrate his strike, Shorty Harris (according to one version of the story) waited until the telegraph and the Tonopah &

LEAD MINE

RHYOLITE

Tidewater Railroad reached Rhyolite, then wired Los Angeles for a carload of whiskey and a carload of eggs. The world's greatest eggnog was Shorty's aim, and he got it. When the train steamed in, fellow townsmen swung axes to knock heads off the whiskey barrels, threw in the eggs shells and all, stirred with their shovels—and drank.

About the same time John Thorndike found the Midas touch gambling in Lone Pine and decided to try in the next town, Rhyolite, three mountain ranges and four valleys to the east. He went. He played. He lost. And when he got back to Lone Pine he regarded neither his ill luck nor his long walk as especially noteworthy.

The boom days were short. In four or five years a market panic scared off investors and the mines closed. Cities and camps were abandoned to the wind and the pack rats. A few became stable communities: Old Man Beatty's ranch grew into a town, and Shoshone stayed as a supply center even after the T&T track was torn up. The minerals of Searles Lake gave rise to Trona. Furnace Creek Ranch switched from alfalfa and beef to dates and tourists.

The boom was over, but the glory days had bred men of a genre too individualistic to die. In the '20s, Walter Scott and Albert Johnson built a castle in Grapevine Canyon simply because they wanted to—hang the illogic of the location! They even built it with eighteen fireplaces and a swimming pool.

In the '40s, Ambroise Aguereberry and Buck Johnston decided they were tired of walking around a hill to their mine each morning, so they drilled and blasted and mucked a tunnel from the bunkhouse door directly into the mine—sixty feet through solid rock, to shortcut a five-minute walk!

In the '50s, a miner up Trail Canyon, left alone to guard camp at Christmas, could stand his guilt no longer and came down one night to confess a murder. A deputy sheriff took him in custody, but on the way to jail the two stopped by the Ranch where a holiday party was underway. By midmorning the next day the deputy was still sleeping it off—and the prisoner drove the paddy wagon to Park Service headquarters and asked what to do!

The spirit of the men ranks as one of the wonders in this valley.

SALT FLATS

SALT PINNACLE

Natural History

GEOLOGY

Time in billions of years is beyond mental grasp, but it is the kind of time that has shaped the earth. The astronomer Jeans expressed it by saying that the entire span of human existence compares to the earth's total age as the thickness of a nickel compares to the height of the Empire State Building. Death Valley has rocks representing all of geologic history, which is estimated at from two to five billion years.

Rocks and Eras: The oldest rocks here form the gray flanks of today's Black Mountains, rising above Badwater as an abrupt wall. They belong to the earth's most ancient era, the Precambrian. In age and character they are similar to the oldest rocks at the bottom of the Grand Canyon.

In places bedding planes are discernible, indicating that much of the rock presently forming the mountain range originated at the bottom of a sea. Life had not yet developed; there are no fossils to help geologists piece together the story. Furthermore, the billions of years have so pressed and twisted and convoluted these rocks that little may ever be known except the fact of their staggering age.

The next oldest era, the Paleozoic, began perhaps five hundred million years ago. (No one can pinpoint these time spans; expert opinion varies and new theories supplant old as fresh studies are undertaken.) Marine fossils begin appearing in rocks of this era. The Funeral and Grapevine mountains are mostly of Paleozoic limestone and dolomites. So are the rocks of Aguereberry Point, in the Panamints.

The third era, the Mesozoic, is represented here by the granites of Cottonwood Canyon, north of the Towne's Pass road, and in the Skidoo and Striped Butte areas of the Panamints. Striped Butte itself, however, is a calico-banded upthrust of Paleozoic sediments.

The Shaping of the Valley: The present era, the Cenozoic, began only about sixty million years ago and so is the easiest to trace. The salt flats, the sand dunes, the shape of the valley itself belong to this era.

The ancestral form of Death Valley was roughed out perhaps as much as eight million years ago, but the shape of the valley as we see it today appeared scarcely over one million years ago. This is exceedingly recent. The whole of the Cenozoic Era represents at most only about one fiftieth of geologic time, and the last one million years represent an equally small fraction of Cenozoic time. Death Valley is geologically young, regardless of how its age strikes the human mind.

Stresses in the earth's crust uplifted the mountains on each side of the valley and dropped the floor in a process of folding and faulting that was neither sudden nor simple, and is not necessarily complete. It is actually a "fault basin" or "graben," not a true valley, which by definition must be cut by stream action. Such fault basins characterize a large part of the California-Nevada desert, but geologists believe Death Valley to be the greatest of them all.

From a structural standpoint Death Valley's floor is as much below sea level as its western rim is above. It does not seem so to the eye because silt and rock eroded from the mountains have stupendously raised the floor. The lowest point in the valley (and in the western hemisphere) is 282 feet below sea level; but the fill beneath this point is almost 10,000 feet thick. Bedrock is found only at that depth below the present surface. From near Badwater to the top of Telescope Peak (11,049 feet), the vertical relief totals almost four miles!

Features to Watch for: So complex is the structural story that one geologist, despairing of untangling it, coined the term "eggbeater formation—some of this, some of that, mixed beyond recognition." Even so, many features are easily distinguished.

There are frequent fault scarps, sudden cliffs caused by fractures and dislocations in the earth's crust. One on the Hanaupah Fan, along the eastern foot of the Panamints, is as much as thirty feet high and two miles long. A smaller but more accessible fault scarp is just east of the Badwater road near Golden Canyon. Synclines and anticlines, "U" shaped bends of strata, show in several canyon walls.

Volcanic activity is represented by Ubehebe Crater and the adjoining craters in the northern valley. Basalt flows formed the Dinosaur, a double-humped black hill that rises from the fan west of Furnace Creek Ranch. Dikes, sharp ridges of volcanic rock, are in several places. One stands like an irregular three-foot wall at Rhodes Well, in the Jubilee Pass area.

Two lakes flooded Death Valley during the Pleistocene period of the present era, the Ice Age. White sediments commonly called the Niter Beds are the main remnants of Lake Rogers, a lake in the north valley.

Lake Manly, a lake in the southern valley estimated to have been six hundred feet deep, left more evidence of its existence. The last of its waters evaporated about ten or fifteen thousand years ago, leaving the salt of Devil's Golfcourse. Beaches cut by its waves show plainly at Shoreline Butte, in the south end of the valley, at Manly Terrace, north of Badwater, and at a point on the Daylight Pass road one and one-half miles northeast of its junction with State 190. The slanting light of early morning and late afternoon accentuates these fragments of the ancient landscape.

The yellow mudhills of Golden Canyon, Zabriskie Point, and Twenty-Mule Team Canyon are the folded and tilted beds of lakes older than Lake Manly. The playas, or dry lakes, of the Racetrack and Bonnie Claire are lake beds much more recent than Lake Manly. Geologic processes seldom belong to one time period and no other. The earth is constantly forming and reforming, and is doing so today at the same pace as always.

Rain runoff produces the alluvial fans that spill onto the valley floor from the canyon mouths. Rock erodes from the mountains, washes down during storms, and accumulates in fan-shaped slopes that cover hundreds of square miles. In the Panamint and Cottonwood mountains the fans are larger than in the Grapevine, Funeral, and Black mountains, indicating that the eastern rim of Death Valley was dislocated more recently than the western rim.

Pale grays and tans streak some fans, marking debris that has recently washed down. On other fans dark tones mark surfaces that have lain undisturbed for so long that they have built up desert varnish.

DANTE'S VIEW

DEVIL'S CORNFIELD

PLANTS

Death Valley National Monument has a great variety of plants, even though as late as 1922 it was reported as "destitute of all vegetation." Two species of orchid grow here, six lilies, ten ferns, and thirty grasses. Twenty-one species of plants are endemic, found here and nowhere else in all the world: they range from goldencarpet and Panamint daisy to Death Valley sage and napkin-ring bush. Springs and streams in the mountains are emerald with watercress.

Growing conditions in the Monument vary too much for it to possibly be unclothed by plants or limited to the stereotype of nothing but cactus. Actually, less than two per cent of the plant species are cactus; but more than fifteen are marsh rushes and reeds. Total plant species identified now number over six hundred.

Distribution and Adaptation: About every two-hundred-foot rise in elevation here means an increase of two-thirds of an inch of precipitation annually and a drop of one degree in temperature—and since elevations in the Monument range from below sea level to over ten thousand feet this means a great variety of growing conditions. So do varying soil conditions: sand lets water sink deep and evaporates it back slowly, but clay and "desert pavement" (close-set stones) cause fast runoff.

The central salt flats are without plants, except possibly for a few primitive species of algae, fungi, and bacteria. At the edge of the salt, where the soil salinity is as high as six per cent, pickleweed and salt grass are able to grow. Their root sap evidently has unusually high osmotic pressure, which keeps them from absorbing too much salt.

Out of the actual salt flats, but close enough to be influenced by them, is a zone characterized by iodine bush and honeysweet. Next come arrow-weed, shadscale, and mesquite, growing where drainage from the canyons floats well enough on top of the salt-saturated subsurface water of the valley to make it usable as fresh water.

Above the mesquite is a wide zone characterized by creosote bush, desert holly, and burrobush. It climbs the fans well into the mountains and merges with sagebrush, blackbrush, and rabbitbush, which in turn give way to pinyon pine and juniper.

For most desert plants water is a problem, first getting it and then conserving it. Roots either go deep or spread wide. Mesquite trees send tap roots as deep as one hundred feet in the sand dunes, and scraggly two-foot saltbushes have roots fifteen or twenty feet long. Cholla cactus solve the problem by the opposite means. Their roots lie just beneath the surface of the ground and radiate in networks thirty feet across.

Most desert plants are low-growing so that water sucked up by the roots can be quickly utilized by the leaves. The shorter the distance between roots and leaves, the less the hazard of transpiration. Furthermore, leaves tend to be small—so much so that the entire leaf surface of an acre of Death Valley plants probably would be less than that of an ordinary-size sycamore tree. Little-leaf ratany, dalea, and burrobush have leaves only a quarter-inch long. Desert tea has mere scales. Cactus has no leaves. The stems are green and have taken over photosynthesis.

Matted hair covers brittlebush leaves, holding back water loss and also insulating against the sun. This is vital, for living protoplasm cannot endure temperatures much above 120°, and when the thermometer soars plants must transpire water to cool themselves.

Mesquite turns its leaves edgewise to the sun during the heat of the day, or folds them to reduce the exposed surface. Cassia drops its leaves during drought. Creosote bush drops its greenest leaves, and has evolved others that can endure greater dehydration than any other leaves in the world.

BEEHIVE CACTUS

Bushes, Cacti, and Trees: Creosote bush is easy to identify. It grows as much as head-high, is lacy, and has shiny leaves and bright yellow flowers which are followed by fuzzy white seedheads. Its roots exude a poison that kills seedlings, chiefly its own. This prevents overcrowding and accounts for much of the widespaced look of the desert.

Common among the scrubby gray bushes are burrobush, brittlebush, cheesebush, dalea, sagebrush, saltbush, and shadscale. Desert holly is the most handsome of the saltbushes, and the easiest to identify. Its scalloped, silvery leaves stay on the year around, and in early spring are interspersed by tiny red buds that look like berries.

The names of several bushes suggest their characteristics. Wetleaf, frequent in washes, is a delight—its leaves are moist to the touch no matter how hot and dry the day. Paperbag bush rattles faintly in a wind because of pods like half-inch papery balloons. Desert fir, a rounded bush and not a tree, has green leaves shaped like the needles of a conifer. The leaves of stingbush bristle with barbed hairs. The stems of cigarette-holder are curiously inflated, and spring straight and conspicuous from ground-hugging mats of leaves.

Botanists have found only fifteen species of cactus in Death Valley National Monument, just two of them truly common—cottontop and beavertail. Cottontop grows in clumps of melon-size heads, occasionally twelve or more together. Indians ate the seeds after freeing them from their protective tufts of cotton; and women straightened the thorns by rubbing them against heated stones, to make awls for use in basketry. Beavertail cactus glows with magenta flowers in spring, a brief surge of brilliance. The pads served as emergency rations for the Indians, not really tasty or nutritious but available if needed (and they often were). Rolling them in sand got rid of the thorns.

Over a dozen trees are native in the Monument, and others such as athel (tamarisk) and date palms are naturalized. Except for mesquite, most of the native trees grow in the mountains. Willows and cottonwoods are common at springs. Joshua trees, unworldly giant lilies, dot the west side of Tin Mountain beyond the Racetrack road, and the Nemo Canyon Flat in the Panamints. Rocky Mountain maple and water birch grow in remote canyons. Mahogany Flat is named for its mountain mahogany.

Pinyon pine and juniper are abundant from about six thousand to eight thousand feet. Above them grow limber and bristlecone pine. Bristlecones three thousand years old have been found on the upper slopes of Telescope Peak; they were sprouting about the time that Solomon began to build the temple in Jerusalem.

Wildflowers: Flowers turn washes and alluvial fans into masses of color as early as January or February in really spectacular wildflower years. In one such year National Park Service naturalists counted one hundred and

JOSHUA TREE, HIDDEN VALLEY

eleven species of flowers between November and March. Daylight Pass and Jubilee Pass usually have the showiest displays.

Amount of rainfall coupled with the temperatures during the rain or immediately afterward determine how well desert annuals germinate and grow. If November and December provide a little over an inch of rain accompanied with temperatures of 46° to 50° F., seeds will sprout. If these conditions are not met seeds will hold over until the next year, or the next, or the next. A delicate balance between growth-stimulating and growth-inhibiting enzymes controls them. Too little rain and the inhibitors are not leached out; temperatures too cool and the stimulators are not triggered.

But when everything is "right," desertgold and sunflower turn roadsides to yellow; gravel ghost floats white and seemingly stemless above the valley floor; phacelia, lupine, paintbrush, mallow, and poppy all tinge the washes with purple, red, and orange. Their ephemeral beauty strikes the human mind as fragile, set as they are amid such harshness. But it is an ordered beauty, operating according to plan.

WILDLIFE

"The shadow of a bird or wild beast never darkens its white glaring sands . . ." a writer in the '70s said of Death Valley. But actually animals range throughout the Monument. A great number "darken the sands" with their shadows, and others, too small for shadows and unacquainted with sand, nonetheless are noteworthy.

A species of water snail (*Asiminea infirma*) lives at Badwater among the roots of iodinebush. It is the only known soft-bodied invertebrate living in a saturated salt solution. Perhaps it came here on the feet of a migrating saltwater bird, for its nearest relative is found at Newport Bay, south of Los Angeles.

A species of fairy shrimp (*Eulimnadia texanus*), whose printed name is about five times as long as the creature itself, lives in the rain-filled tinajas of Death Valley Buttes. They are translucent, a quarter-inch long, and fringed under their bellies by myriad swimmerettes. In summer they disappear, but when winter comes they are back. The adults die when the water evaporates from the tiny hollows that are their entire world, but their eggs hold over until the new season's rain releases the life within them.

Schools of inch-long fish swim in Salt Creek, the Amargosa River, and Saratoga Springs: they are three separate species of *Cyprinodons*, or "pupfish." Like the shrimp and the snails, they are unknown anywhere else in the world. Their ancestors evidently lived in Lake Manly, and as it dried at the close of the Ice Age the fish managed to adjust from life in an enormous, cold, freshwater lake to life in small, isolated, warm, and increasingly salty creeks and springs. (Salt Creek is 1.9 per cent salt, about six times as salty as the ocean.)

The Problem of Water: Water is crucial for desert animals. They need it for vital bodily processes, as does all life everywhere, and they need it for cooling.

Heat is a killer, yet many animals cannot reduce their body temperature by sweating, as man does. The best a kangaroo rat can do is dribble saliva onto its breast and get what cooling it can from the evaporation. An overheated horned toad can only loll out its pink tongue and pant, squandering body water to cool tissues.

Water is too precious to place needless demands upon the supply. Animals therefore avoid fatal rises in body temperature by avoiding circumstances that lead to them. Lizards streak across the ground on their toes, then survey the world from the shade of a bush. Some rodents burrow to escape the heat of day; others estivate, the summer equivalent of winter hibernation. Bighorn sheep and mule deer stay in the mountains where even summer days are relatively cool.

Some animals depend on drinking water regularly and copiously. The burros that run wild in the Panamints and Cottonwoods (descended from

PACK RAT

prospectors' burros) can go four days without water, then suck up enough in half an hour to last them another four days. Coyotes can smell underground water and dig sloping four- or five-foot tunnels to reach it.

Kitfox get much of their needed moisture from the blood of their prey. Grasshopper mice depend on the moisture in the insects they eat (insects are from sixty to eighty-five per cent water). Ground squirrels, jackrabbits, and pack rats lap dew and feed on succulent green plants.

Pocket mice and kangaroo rats manage on a diet solely of dry seeds. Their systems are geared to get along exclusively on metabolic water, the water produced by the oxidation of food. (One gram of carbohydrate yields about one-half gram of water when oxidized.) The metabolic processes of all mammals, including man, produce such water; but pocket mice and kangaroo rats are unusual in utilizing this single source of water. They do not drink even when rain puddles wet the desert floor, nor do they supplement their diet with green plants.

Animals to Watch for: Lizards are all about. Gridiron-tailed lizards dash across the highway with their tails arched high over their backs; brown swifts dart from underfoot; whiptails snap up ants with their long tongues. Chuckawallas are the largest lizards in the Monument, measuring twelve or more inches long. They have the curious defensive habit of running into a crevice and blowing themselves up into such a tight fit that no amount of an enemy's tugging can dislodge them. The Gecko lizard has pink-brown, translucent skin, yellow eyes with vertical slits like a cat's, and a thin tongue with which it "licks its chops" after gulping down a fly or moth. It also can squeak when annoyed; it is the only American lizard with a voice.

About eighteen species of snakes are found in the Monument, but none of them are likely to be seen. A rattler sunning on a rock or a sidewinder

GECKO

CHUCKAWALLA

resting half-buried in the sand of a wash will escape if possible when disturbed; if startled, however, they may strike, with or without the buzzing of their tails.

These are the only two poisonous creatures in Death Valley. No lizards here are poisonous, nor are any insects or the related scorpions, centipedes, and spiders, except for black widow spiders. Most likely to actually cause misery are the inch-long, bloodsucking horseflies!

Desert mammals generally forage and hunt at night. A campfire occasionally catches the gleam in the eyes of kitfox drawn by curiosity to the edge of the light, or of kangaroo rats leaping over the sand in search of dinner. A car's headlights may pick up the fleeting form of a bobcat or ringtail.

Of the fifty mammal species on the Death Valley checklist, over half are mice, rats, ground squirrels, and rabbits. Another sixteen per cent are bats.

Among the larger animals, bighorn sheep are perhaps of the greatest concern. They now are estimated at over one thousand head, making Death Valley one of the last strongholds of their kind. How long it will remain so depends on man, for man is a greater threat by far to sheep than the preying of mountain lions or the competition of burros for food and water.

Every year of this century one species of animal has disappeared forever from the earth, driven into oblivion by man. For while some creatures can manage a furtive sharing of the land, others cannot. Bighorn are too frightened by man to share grazing land and watering places with him and no new territory is left for them to move into. They now depend on about forty of the three hundred fresh-water springs and seeps in the Monument. Whether these forty remain wild will determine the future of the bighorn sheep here.

Birds: A ranger patrolling the valley in summer once found a great blue heron hunched forlornly beneath the overflow drip of the cooler at Stove

Pipe Wells Hotel. Campers at Saratoga Springs have awakened to the squabbling of hundreds of coots. Whistling swans used to paddle sedately in the ponds at Furnace Creek Ranch, and swimmers at the Inn have shared the pool with grebes.

Death Valley's resident and migrant birds number nearly three hundred species. As many as 1,342 individuals of 44 species have been counted in a single day within a 15-mile radius.

One of the best places to watch for birds is the athel and mesquite thickets near Furnace Creek Ranch and the marsh behind the golf course. Any day from September to May is likely to disclose flickers, larks, sparrows, phoebes, kinglets, shrikes, pipits, robins, doves, bluebirds, warblers, swallows, teal, snipe, killdeer, and many others.

Ravens, redtails, marsh hawks, and occasionally golden eagles circle overhead. Roadrunners sprint after lizards. Snowy egrets, arctic loons, and bufflehead ducks sometimes settle for a night or two. Even cormorants and wood ibis are known.

One-third of the bird species found in Death Valley have been recorded in midsummer—but the heat often brings disaster. White-fronted geese have been found dead on the salt flats, evidently having mistaken them for water and come in to rest. Tree swallows have been seen prostrate and panting beneath the trees at Furnace Creek Ranch. A redwing blackbird once was found mummified, its claws still gripping the twig of a shrub and its wings open as if seeking flight.

WILD BURROS   **BIGHORN SHEEP**

NEAR KEANE WONDER

Weather

The Death Valley weather story is more than blazing heat. Winters are delightful and even in summer when the valley floor is simmering the bordering mountain ranges are comfortable. Men have died here of heat and thirst, but they also have died by drowning and freezing, for thunderstorms flood the canyons and snowstorms shroud the mountains.

Temperatures: In summer the ground feels hot even through thick shoe soles, an automobile fender is burning to the touch, paper turns brittle, glued joints in tables and chairs dry and come apart, corks shrink and fall into bottles.

Official temperature readings are made from thermometers housed in standard, white, louvered boxes set five feet above the ground. These readings show that every month from May to October has topped 120° at least once, and all except December and January have been above 90°.

One year (1959) maximum readings were 100° or more every day from May 30 to September 12 except for one day which reached only 99°. Another year (1913) there were two unbroken weeks of 120° and above. Sometimes even minimums fail to drop below the 100° mark!

Death Valley's record high is 134°, the reading of July 10, 1913. "I remember the day very distinctly," wrote the Superintendent of Furnace Creek Ranch years later. "A man by the name of Busch perished in the valley north of the ranch that day on account of the heat. It was blowing very hard."

For a few years 134° stood as the world's highest temperature; then the station at Azizia, Libya, recorded 136°. Even so, meteorologists regard Death Valley as the hottest place in the world. Temperatures at Badwater average four degrees above those at Furnace Creek (which would boost the record 134° to 138°) and the valley's overall summer maximums consistently exceed those anywhere else in the world. July highs for the last fifty years average 116° and August highs 114°. This is ten per cent above the mean maximums for Azizia.

THERMOMETER SHELTER, FURNACE CREEK

Ground temperatures tend to be about fifty per cent higher than air temperatures. A reading of 190° was made at Tule Spring in July 1958, the highest official reading ever made in Death Valley—and significant because it is ground temperature, not air temperature at five feet, that plants and animals must contend with.

By contrast, winter temperatures are mild. From November through March midday temperatures are typically in the 60's or 70's, with nights dropping into the 40's. Occasionally it freezes. One January (1937) the temperature dropped below freezing each night for three weeks, but the total January minimums over a thirty-year period average only three freezes per January.

In 1913, the year of the 134° record high, the record low also was reached: on the night of January 8 the mercury dropped to 15°. This makes a January-to-July temperature range of 119°.

Humidity and Rain: No prolonged study of relative humidity has been made in Death Valley, but occasional checks indicate that in July it approaches zero. Readings of two and three per cent are quite frequent, although they more often range from about five to twenty per cent.

When rain falls in summer the heat of the ground drives most of the moisture immediately back into the air. Within an hour the temperature has been known to drop thirty degrees and the relative humidity to climb seventy percentage points.

Rainfall averages one and one-half inches per year at Furnace Creek, the lowest average rainfall in the United States. Only twice in fifty years has it exceeded four inches, and fifteen months once passed without so much as a measurable trace of rain. Sometimes gray streamers of rain trail from overhead clouds but fail to reach the ground. The hot air sucks them dry before they get that far.

Other times rain does reach the ground—and with disastrous results. A cloudburst in July 1950 cut six feet into the Furnace Creek road in some places and blanketed it beneath four feet of mud in other places. Water eight feet deep roared past Furnace Creek Inn, ripping out creosote bushes and rolling boulders the size of a bathtub. At the Ranch 0.7 inch of rain was recorded; five miles north 0.08 inch fell.

Cloudbursts typically unload a great quantity of water very quickly in a localized area. Runoff is prodigious—and here where the total runoff of an entire mountain catchment basin must funnel through a narrow canyon

STORM CLOUDS, DANTE'S VIEW

SNOW IN THE PANAMINTS

onto the valley floor, devastation is frequent. The Titus Canyon road washes out almost every summer. And in Surprise Canyon prospectors once worked intermittently for eighteen years to rebuild the road to Panamint City, finishing it in time to drive a truck to their mine exactly twice before a cloudburst took it out again.

Snow usually whitens Telescope Peak and the crest of the Panamints from December to May. Drifts pile twenty feet deep, and the roads over Towne's Pass and Harrisburg Flat sometimes must be closed. Snow occasionally blows across the valley floor from mountain storms. The flakes usually melt as soon as they land, but once in a while three or four inches cover the ground, burying small plants and curiously festooning the larger ones.

DESERT SURVIVAL

Men need quantities of water under conditions such as are typical in summer here. The body's only way to keep cool when the air temperature is above skin temperature (92°) is by sweating. A man driving a car on a 110° day may sweat almost one quart of water an hour, and the only way he can make up this water loss is by drinking an equivalent amount. There is no way to get along on less water by "training." Men who have dehydrated themselves in scientific experiments had to drink just as much water to restore normal hydration after the twentieth time as after the first.

Thirst is a signal of actual body need, not merely of discomfort. It is the first symptom of dehydration. If it is not relieved, a general slowing down and loss of appetite soon follow; then fever and sleepiness. Dehydration equivalent to a five per cent loss of body weight brings on nausea; six to ten per cent produces dizziness, difficulty in breathing, and tingling in the arms and legs. The heart beats hard, pumping blood which has thickened because of the water lost from the body. Walking becomes impossible. A fifteen to twenty per cent dehydration generally is fatal.

However, given water, even a man who has collapsed will quickly rehydrate. Furthermore, no harm comes from gulping it quickly, although under such conditions icewater may cause temporary stomach cramps.

What if there isn't any water, or not enough? Research in the last few years has supplied definite answers to replace the old tales.

Clothes should be kept on, to hold down the rate of sweat evaporation. A man may be cooler with his shirt off, but when water is limited the important thing is to avoid any increase in sweat demand, regardless of immediate comfort. Over twenty per cent of the body's water loss can be prevented simply by staying clothed.

Keeping in the shade during the daytime saves fifteen per cent; resting instead of walking saves about forty per cent. Lying down eases the burden on the heart, but it should be done off the ground. Temperatures only one foot above the ground are as much as forty-five degrees cooler than at the surface. By observing such precautions a man without water can expect to survive two days at 120° maximum temperature. With two and one-half gallons he could survive three days; with five gallons, four days or more.

If walking is necessary it should be done only at night, with the start delayed long enough after sunset for the temperature to really have dropped. (However, walking seldom is wise. Motorists should stay with their cars until help comes.)

Nothing should be eaten except perhaps a little candy because digestion diverts water that otherwise would be available for sweat. Drinking alcohol, blood, or urine will only increase dehydration, although these liquids may be used to wet clothes and thereby reduce the need to evaporate sweat for a time. Soft drinks, fruit juice, and other beverages of course are suitable to drink; they are essentially water.

Salt tablets should never be taken without ample water. Heavy sweating produces a slight salt loss from body tissue, but a sudden excess of salt without sufficient water to handle it can cause serious distress and further reduce the amount of body moisture available as sweat. The best way to handle the need for salt during hot weather is to use a little extra on food.

In the old days death by exposure was not uncommon in this valley. At least thirty-two such deaths occurred in ten years during the turn-of-the-century mining boom. But times have changed. Good roads and fast cars have replaced unknown routes and plodding burros. Park Service rangers make daily patrols. Tens of thousands of people now cross Death Valley in midsummer simply to see what it is like.

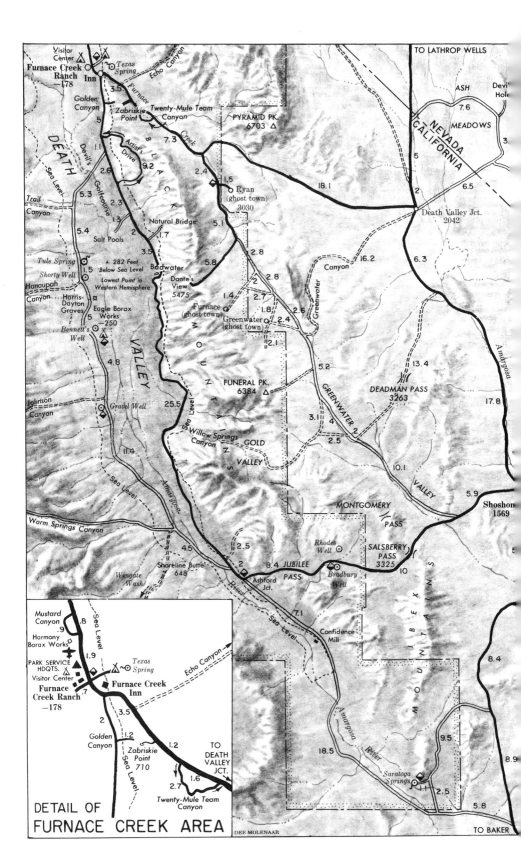

TO LATHROP WELLS

Visitor
Center
Furnace Creek
Ranch
-178
*Texas
Spring*
3.5
ASH
Devi
Hole
7.6
MEADOWS
NEVADA
CALIFORNIA
Golden
Canyon
Zabriskie
Point
Twenty-Mule Team
Canyon
5
7.3
Furnace
Creek
5
3.
DEATH
Devil's
1.1
Artist's
Drive
2.6
9.2
2.4
1.5
Ryan
(ghost town)
3030
18.1
2
Death Valley Jct.
2042
Sea Level
5.3
Trail
Canyon
Golfcourse
2.3
1.3
Natural Bridge
5.1
B
L
A
C
K
2.8
16.2
Canyon
6.3
5.4
Salt Pools
1.7
3.5
5.8
2.8
Tule Spring
1.5
Shorty Well
282 Feet
Below Sea Level
Lowest Point in
Western Hemisphere
Badwater
Dante's
View
5475
2
2.7
2.8
Greenwater
Canyon
Hanaupah
Canyon
Harris-
Dayton
Graves
Eagle Borax
Works
-250
1.4
Furnace
(ghost town)
1.8
2.6
Greenwater
(ghost town)
2.4
Amargosa
Bennett's
Well
5
2.1
VALLEY
4.8
FUNERAL PK.
6384
5.2
13.4
DEADMAN PASS
3263
M
O
U
N
T
A
I
N
S
17.8
Johnson
Canyon
Gravel Well
25.5
Sea Level
3.11
GREENWATER
4
2
11.4
Willow Springs
Canyon
GOLD
VALLEY
2.5
VALLEY
10.1
Amargosa
MONTGOMERY
PASS
5.9
Shoshon
1569
Warm Springs Canyon
4.5
2.5
Rhodes
Well
SALSBERRY
PASS
3325
10
Shoreline Butte
648
2
8.4
JUBILEE
PASS
Ashford
Jct.
Bradbury
Well
Wingate
Wash
River
7.1
Sea Level
Confidence
Mill
I
B
E
X
8.4

M
O
U
N
T
A
I
N
S

Amargosa

River

18.5

9.5

8.9

Saratoga
Springs

2.5

5.8

TO BAKER

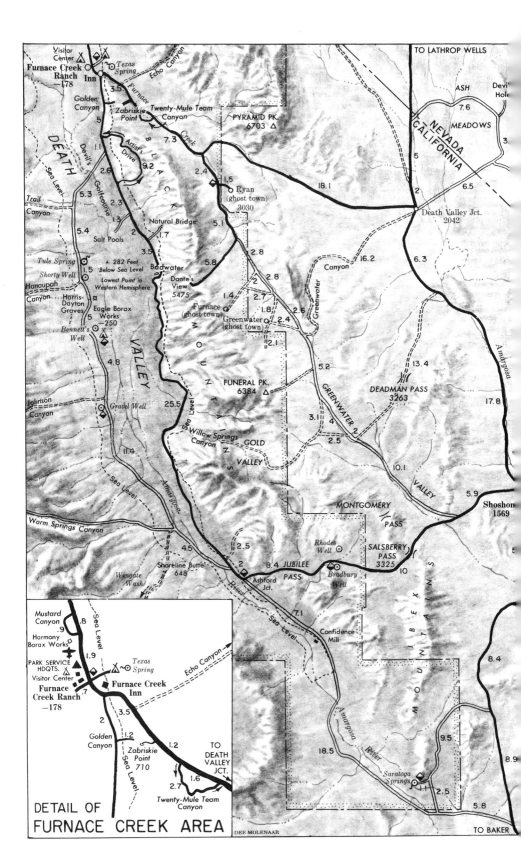

DETAIL OF
FURNACE CREEK AREA

Mustard
Canyon
.8
Sea Level
.9
Harmony
Borax Works
1.9
PARK SERVICE
HDQTS.
Visitor Center
*Texas
Spring*
Echo Canyon
Furnace
Creek Ranch
-178
.7
Furnace Creek
Inn
3.5
2
Golden
Canyon
1.2
1.2
Zabriskie
Point
710
Sea Level
TO
DEATH
VALLEY
JCT.
2.7
1.6
Twenty-Mule Team
Canyon

DEE MOLENAAR

WHERE TO STAY
HOSTELRIES: Furnace Creek Inn, Furnace Creek Ranch, Shoshone, Death Valley Junction.
CAMPGROUNDS: Bennett's Well, Furnace Creek, Texas Spring.

FOOD AND GASOLINE
Furnace Creek, Shoshone, Death Valley Junction.

WATER
DRINKING WATER: Furnace Creek, Shoshone, Death Valley Junction; *Purify before drinking:* Bradbury Well, Gravel Well, Saratoga Springs.
RADIATOR WATER: Ashford Junction, Ryan Junction.

RANGER STATION
Furnace Creek, Rhodes Well (winter only).

WHAT TO DO
MUSEUMS: National Park Visitor Center, Furnace Creek; Borax Museum, Furnace Creek Village.
TALKS: Illustrated introduction to Death Valley, daily, at the Visitor Center, every hour on the hour; naturalist program every evening, in season, Visitor Center.
CONDUCTED TOURS (nature walks, auto caravans, horseback rides): Ask for schedules of current National Park Service and Furnace Creek Ranch activities.
QUICK TRIPS: Golden Canyon, short and narrow; the adobe ruins of Harmony Borax Works; Twenty-Mule Team Canyon, with its labyrinthine mudhills; Zabriskie Point, ancient lake beds now sharply eroded.
HALF-DAY TRIPS: The colorful hills and cliffs of Artist's Drive; Badwater, low point in the western hemisphere; Dante's View for the panorama; Devil's Golfcourse for the salt formations.
ALL-DAY TRIPS: Greenwater Valley, sites of ghost towns; Jubilee Pass, beautiful drive along the base of the Black Mountains; West Side, a little-traveled graded road.
HIKES: Out into the valley floor from Badwater; along the skyline at Dante's View; the Haystacks beyond Harmony Borax Works; Natural Bridge Canyon; Red Cathedral and Gower Gulch in Golden Canyon.

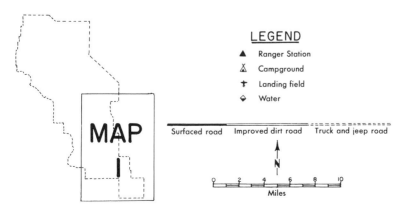

LEGEND
▲ Ranger Station
𝕏 Campground
✝ Landing field
◇ Water

Surfaced road Improved dirt road Truck and jeep road

MAP
1

N

0 2 4 6 8 10
Miles

MAP 1. FURNACE CREEK TO BADWATER AND DANTE'S VIEW

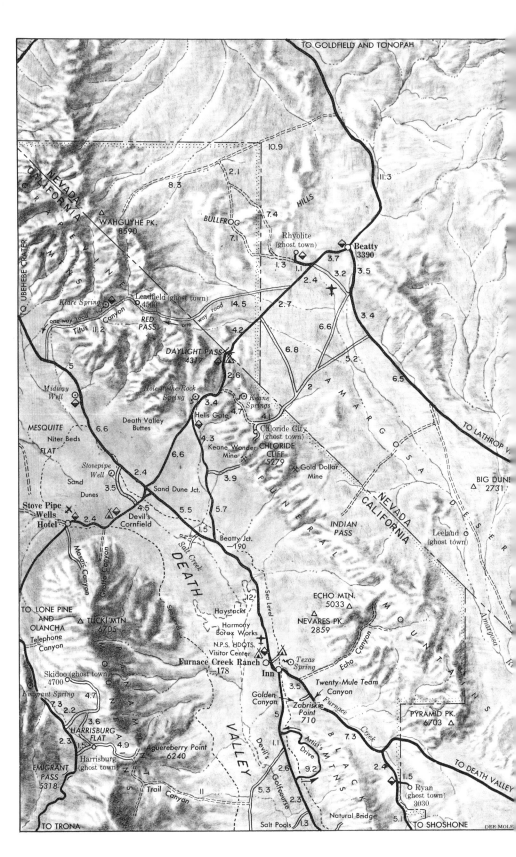

WHERE TO STAY
HOSTELRIES: Beatty, Furnace Creek Inn and Ranch, Stove Pipe Wells Hotel.
CAMPGROUNDS: Furnace Creek, Midway Well, Sand Dunes, Texas Spring.

FOOD AND GASOLINE
Beatty, Furnace Creek, Stove Pipe Wells Hotel.

WATER
DRINKING WATER: Beatty, Furnace Creek, Rhyolite, Stove Pipe Wells Hotel; *Purify before drinking:* Daylight Pass, Klare Spring, Midway Well.
RADIATOR WATER: Hell's Gate, Mud Canyon, Ryan Junction, 5 miles west of Stove Pipe Wells Hotel.

RANGER STATION
Furnace Creek.

WHAT TO DO
MUSEUMS: National Park Visitor Center; Borax Museum; both Furnace Creek.
TALKS: Illustrated introduction to Death Valley, daily, at the Visitor Center, every hour on the hour; naturalist program every evening, in season, Visitor Center; frequent evening programs, in season, Stove Pipe Wells Hotel.
CONDUCTED TOURS (nature walks, auto caravans, horseback rides): National Park Service, Furnace Creek Ranch, and Stove Pipe Wells Hotel.
QUICK TRIPS: Golden Canyon, short and narrow; the adobe ruins of Harmony Borax Works; Mosaic Canyon, for water-polished walls; Salt Creek, for flowing water and abundant wildlife; the Sand Dunes; Twenty-Mule Team Canyon, labyrinthine mudhills; Zabriskie Point, ancient lake beds now sharply eroded.
HALF-DAY TRIPS: The warm mineral springs (not potable) and mine ruins of Keane Wonder; the ghost town of Rhyolite; the high view of Chloride Cliff.
ALL-DAY TRIP: Titus Canyon, with the ghost town of Leadfield and the twisting narrows at its mouth.
HIKES: The Haystacks out from Harmony Borax Works; up the tramway trail or along the base of the mountains at Keane Wonder; through the lower part of Mosaic Canyon, and as far beyond as time permits; Salt Creek, along both the stream and the crest of the hills; the Sand Dunes; Red Cathedral and Gower Gulch in Golden Canyon.

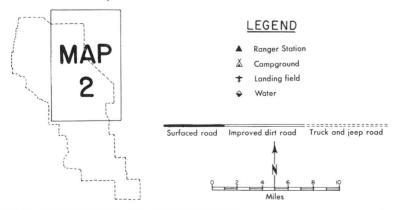

MAP 2

LEGEND
▲ Ranger Station
⚊ Campground
✦ Landing field
◆ Water

Surfaced road   Improved dirt road   Truck and jeep road

0   2   4   6   8   10
Miles

N

MAP 2. DAYLIGHT PASS TO SCOTTY'S CASTLE

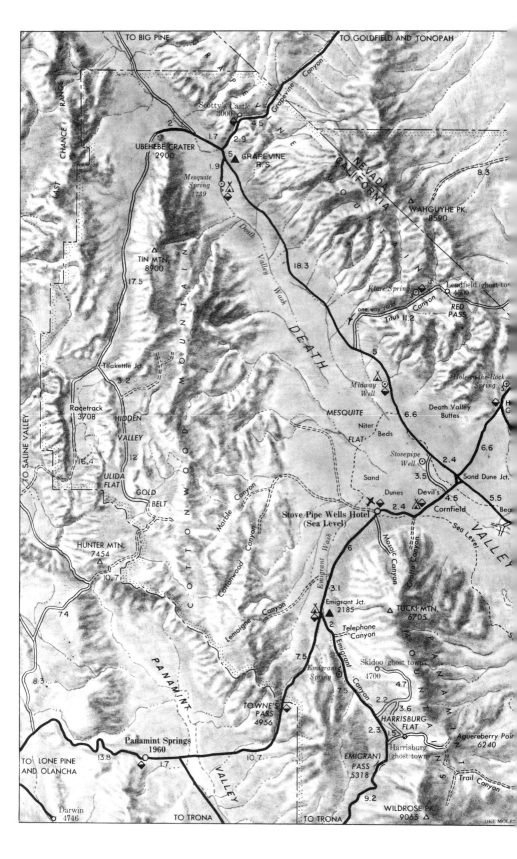

WHERE TO STAY
HOSTELRIES: Stove Pipe Wells Hotel.
CAMPGROUNDS: Emigrant Junction, Mesquite Spring, Midway Well, Sand Dunes.

FOOD AND GASOLINE
Panamint Springs, Scotty's Castle, Stove Pipe Wells Hotel.

WATER
DRINKING WATER: Emigrant Junction, Grapevine Ranger Station, Mesquite Spring, Panamint Springs, Scotty's Castle, Stove Pipe Wells Hotel; *Purify before drinking:* Emigrant Spring, Klare Spring, Midway Well.
RADIATOR WATER: 5 miles west of Stove Pipe Wells Hotel, Towne's Pass.

RANGER STATIONS
Emigrant, Grapevine.

WHAT TO DO
TALKS: Evenings twice weekly, in season, at Stove Pipe Wells Hotel.
CONDUCTED TOURS: Scotty's Castle, hourly in season, and according to demand out of season; ask for current schedule of activities at Stove Pipe Wells Hotel.
QUICK TRIPS: Mosaic Canyon, for its water-polished rock walls; the Sand Dunes, accessible either from State Highway 190 or the graded road to Stove Pipe Well.
HALF-DAY TRIPS: The view of Death Valley from Aguereberry Point; Scotty's Castle, the mansion of Albert Johnson and Walter Scott; Skidoo, turn-of-the-century boom town, now a ghost town.
ALL-DAY TRIPS: The Racetrack, for a back-country drive to the site of the mysterious "Moving Rocks" (vehicles prohibited on playa surface, but all right to walk); Ubehebe Crater, one of a series of volcanic explosion pits.
HIKES: Through the lower part of Mosaic Canyon, and as far beyond as time permits; the Sand Dunes; around the rim of Ubehebe Crater and to the other craters beyond.

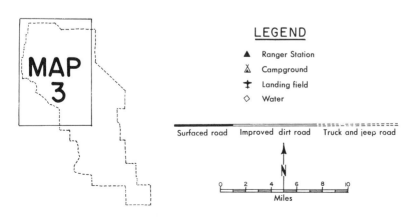

LEGEND

▲ Ranger Station
Ⓧ Campground
✝ Landing field
◇ Water

Surfaced road   Improved dirt road   Truck and jeep road

0 2 4 6 8 10
Miles

MAP 3. STOVE PIPE WELLS TO UBEHEBE CRATER

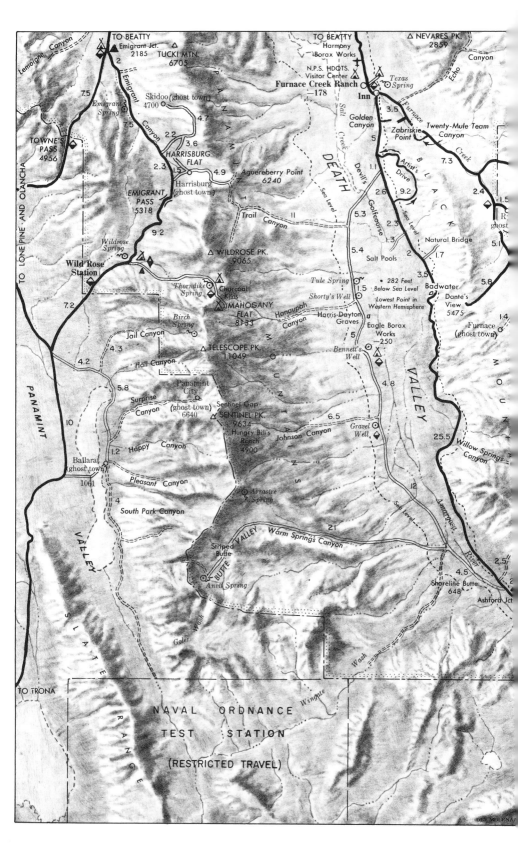

WHERE TO STAY
HOSTELRY: Wild Rose Station.
CAMPGROUNDS: Mahogany Flat, Thorndike, Wildrose.

FOOD AND GASOLINE
Trona, Wild Rose Station.

WATER
DRINKING WATER: Trona, Wild Rose Station, Wildrose Campground, Wildrose
Ranger Station; *Purify before drinking:* Emigrant Spring, Thorndike (unavail-
able in winter owing to freezing).
RADIATOR WATER: Towne's Pass, Wildrose entrance road.

RANGER STATION
Wild Rose, Emigrant.

WHAT TO DO
HALF-DAY TRIPS: Aguereberry Point, for the view of Death Valley; the ghost town
of Skidoo, turn-of-the-century gold mining camp.
ALL-DAY TRIPS: Ghost town of Ballarat at the base of the Panamint Mountains in
Panamint Valley; the stone Charcoal Kilns in upper Wildrose Canyon; Mahogany
Flat on the crest of the Panamint Mountains.
HIKES: Telescope Peak, either all the way to the top or simply a sample of the
trail, for the view and the pines; best from April through November (trail is snow-
covered in winter; hazardous).

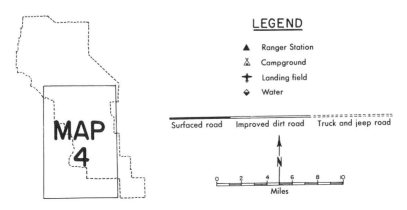

LEGEND

▲ Ranger Station
⚑ Campground
✈ Landing field
◈ Water

Surfaced road   Improved dirt road   Truck and jeep road

N

0   2   4   6   8   10
Miles

MAP 4. THE PANAMINT MOUNTAINS

Sights on Main Roads

What to see is partly a matter of time—time of day as well as the hours available. Long shadows enhance some views; with others the angle of light is relatively unimportant. Consider too that sunshine comes earlier in the morning to the west side of the valley than to the east, and conversely that it lingers later in the day along the base of the Funeral and Black mountains than along the Panamints. As for weather, try the high country if the day is hot; the valley floor if it is cold; the canyons if there is wind, drizzle, or haze (because of their protection and close-in views).

Tours suggested here introduce major points of interest accessible primarily by paved road; check the maps to pinpoint locations. For current road information ask at the National Park Service Visitor Center at Furnace Creek or at any ranger station. Be sure to start out with ample gasoline and water. The miles between supplies are long.

ON THE WAY TO BADWATER (Map 1)

Tour: Past the FAULT SCARP; up GOLDEN CANYON; over to the DEVIL'S GOLF-COURSE and SALT POOLS; south to the TURTLEBACK; and BADWATER (16½ miles south of Furnace Creek).

Side Trips: NATURAL BRIDGE; ARTIST'S DRIVE.

Possible Loop Trip: South from BADWATER, then return either by the unpaved WEST SIDE road or up JUBILEE and SALSBERRY PASSES and on to State 190 via SHOSHONE or the unpaved GREENWATER cutoff.

Suggested Time: Two to four hours, preferably in the afternoon for best light in the canyons; longer if plans include a stroll in Golden Canyon or at Natural Bridge, or a loop trip beyond Badwater.

Look for the FAULT SCARP 1 mile south of Furnace Creek Inn. It is a two- to six-foot bank just east of the road—not striking to the eye but worth noticing because it marks an abrupt lowering of the valley floor by block faulting, the prime earth force that shaped Death Valley.

A mile farther south, GOLDEN CANYON threads among the mudhills, a narrow canyon, its walls sheer and glowing "gold" when touched by the setting sun. The red clay that patches the mouth of the canyon was a source of face

BADWATER

paint for the Indians. They called it, and because of it the whole central valley, *dumbisha*. But the word came to be spelled "tomesha" in English and mistranslated as "Ground Afire"—romantic, compared to "Face Paint," but without basis.

Two short trails lead beyond the end of the road (1½ miles up the canyon): one goes to a colorful natural amphitheater called RED CATHEDRAL; the other heads up GOWER GULCH to the foot of MANLY BEACON, a pinnacle of golden clay. Park at the end of the road only. Allow a half hour for each hike. There are ladders to climb on the Red Cathedral trail, but easy strolling up Gower Gulch.

The spur road (1½ miles) to the DEVIL'S GOLFCOURSE and SALT POOLS is about 11 miles south of Golden Canyon. Rock-hard salt, which is almost pure sodium chloride (the same as table salt), crusts over the mud that fills this part of the valley. It formed by capillary action as a shallow lake evaporated about two thousand years ago. Salt was drawn up by the evaporating water, then crystallized into a jumble of sharp spires and ridges as much as two feet high. The entire salt pan covers two hundred square miles of the valley floor and has three separate zones of salt, owing to the varying solubility of different types of salt. As the lake dried, its carbonates (baking soda) precipitated first, at the edge of the present salt pan. Next the sulfates (Epsom salt) precipitated, followed by the chlorides.

The SALT POOLS are depressions in the salt crust two or three feet deep and up to eight feet across. They are often dry, unless recent rain has raised

NATURAL
BRIDGE

the subsurface water table. The best place to look for them is one quarter of a mile west from the end of the road. There is no trail; pick a route through the salt. Listen for a tinkling sound as the pinnacles expand and contract in response to changing air temperatures.

Notice the rounded, bare thrust of the mountain wall just north of Badwater. This is the TURTLEBACK, a fault scarp formed in the same way as the small one near Golden Canyon, but scaled gigantically—appropriate to the wrenching dislocation that occurred here as the valley floor slipped thousands of feet down this rock face.

BADWATER, 279.8 feet below sea level, was thought to be the lowest point in the western hemisphere until 1951, when men with the U.S. Geological Survey mapping west of Badwater found two points that are −282 feet. (Neither spot is distinguishable to the eye, or marked by a sign.)

Only two continents in the world have land lower than this: Africa, with the Qattara Depression, −440 feet, and Asia, with the Dead Sea, −1,290 feet. Even so, those who relish superlatives can argue that Death Valley is unique because a relatively loose fill of rock and silt 7,000 to 10,000 feet thick rests on bedrock, so that the surface of the land is far above its structural base. Stripped of this fill, the floor of the valley would be by far the lowest land surface in the world.

The name Badwater comes from an early-day surveyor's candid notation on his map when his mule refused to drink here. Much of the water in Death Valley is "bad" because of salts; but it is not poisonous, as prospectors violently ill from Epsom and Glaubers salts were apt to believe.

A half-hour's walk west of Badwater leads among mud "saucers" six feet across, rimmed by salt. There is no trail; wear old shoes.

A 2-mile unpaved spur road north of Badwater leads to NATURAL BRIDGE. The road is steeper than it seems and cars often overheat.

The bridge is one quarter of a mile up the canyon from the head of the fan. It arches fifty feet above the wash, long ago undercut by water and left spanning the canyon. Beyond it, look for a great chute where water drops over the canyon rim and cuts into the wall, and farther on notice where half a dozen spillways have cut a grotto seventy-five feet into the canyon wall. Watch for water-cut "benches" along the sides of the canyon. They indicate former levels of the wash.

ARTIST'S DRIVE, winding 9½ miles through washes and mudhills, is a one-way road entered from the south. It is paved, but narrow and with occasional sharp curves and steep grades. The entrance is 7½ miles north of Badwater.

The fan climbs steadily above the valley floor, offering an increasingly sweeping view back across the salt flats. Ahead, clay hills lie one on top of another, streaked and stabbed with color caused by the oxidation of iron-bearing minerals—"rust" at its most beautiful, in tints of red, orange, yellow, green, and purple, offset by black and buff. Late afternoon light is best for photographs; ARTIST'S PALETTE, midway through the drive, is the best single vantage point.

FURNACE CREEK TO DANTE'S VIEW (Map 1)

Tour: HARMONY BORAX WORKS and MUSTARD CANYON; the MUSEUMS; up FURNACE CREEK WASH to ZABRISKIE POINT; through TWENTY-MULE TEAM CANYON; on to DANTE'S VIEW (24 miles southeast of Furnace Creek).

Side Trips: RYAN; GREENWATER.

Possible Loop Trip: Through GREENWATER VALLEY after leaving Dante's View and back to Death Valley by SALSBERRY and JUBILEE passes, or via SHOSHONE and DEATH VALLEY JUNCTION.

Suggested Time: Three or four hours; morning is generally favored.

Today silence blankets HARMONY BORAX WORKS (1 mile north of Furnace Creek Ranch), but from 1882 to 1887 the air rang with the sound of men and mules. Forty men worked here refining borax, which they shipped by twenty-mule team to the railhead at Mojave—a 165-mile trip calling for ten overnight camps, about half of them without water. The refining process consisted basically of heating vats of "cottonball" borates mixed with water and carbonated soda, then cooling the resulting liquor in tanks where the borax crystallized on suspended iron rods. The old boiler and vats are all that remain now, along with adobe walls washing back into the desert and low mounds of borax lining the valley floor beyond.

Over fifty industries use borax. It is used in fertilizers, repellents, and preservatives; laundry preparations; porcelain enamels, ceramics, and glass; and serves as a flux in metallurgy.

North of the old borax plant the road winds for one half mile through MUSTARD CANYON. Oxidizing iron has colored the mudhills yellow; bentonite clay, alternately swelling when wet and shrinking while drying, has sculptured their slopes into a strange fretwork; salt adds the look of snow.

Museum displays and hourly slide talks at the National Park Service Visitor Center present information on the history and natural history of

HARMONY BORAX WORKS

ZABRISKIE POINT

Death Valley. At Furnace Creek Ranch another museum and an outdoor display of equipment trace the story of borax mining. Both museums and all displays and services are free.

FURNACE CREEK WASH divides the Amargosa Range into the Black Mountains on the south and the Funerals on the north. A mile up the wash is TRAVERTINE SPRING, the first spring that the '49ers found after thirsty days crossing the Amargosa Desert. The water now is used for domestic purposes and irrigation at the Inn and Ranch, and until the 1960's it also furnished power—for hydroelectric plants were the rule in Death Valley despite its reputation of utter dryness. Actually, flowing water was easy to come by compared to gasoline for engine-driven generators!

ZABRISKIE POINT is named for Christian Brevoort Zabriskie, an early-day head of borax operations. Below the parking area stretch ancient lakebeds, now up-ended into a mass of sharply eroded yellow mudhills. Early morning and late afternoon light are best. If transportation can be arranged, try walking from Zabriskie Point past Manly Beacon and to the road at the head of Golden Canyon.

A mile above Zabriskie Point is the entrance to TWENTY-MULE TEAM CANYON, a 4½-mile graded road that climbs and dips among bare, weathering hills. (It is a one-way drive; enter from the downhill end.) Borax was mined in this canyon but never freighted through it by twenty-mule teams. The first frame house in Death Valley, a boardinghouse for miners, was built midway through the canyon. Moved to Furnace Creek Ranch, it now houses the Borax Museum.

Listen for sounds of the hills expanding and contracting with changes in temperature (especially noticeable in midmorning and midafternoon). Walk to the top of one of the hills to sense the full desolation of bare, eroded clay stretching into the distance, backdropped by the rock mass of the Panamints and the Funerals. If possible, sample the remorseless glare of midday here; then come again and see the contrast when shadows signal the beginning or end of the day.

DANTE'S VIEW overlooks Death Valley directly above Badwater. The salt flats stretch as a carpet of white more than a mile below; beyond them the Panamint Mountains rise as a wall culminating in Telescope Peak (11,049 feet, more than a mile higher than Dante's View); and on the horizon are the Sierra Nevada Mountains, with Mount Whitney, at 14,495 feet, the highest peak in the United States outside of Alaska. The mesquite thickets at the springs along the west side of Death Valley show as small dark green spots; the alluvial fans above them look smooth and even, although actually washes fifty feet deep corrugate them. Sunrise and sunset are spectacular at Dante's View. Walk along the crest of the mountains, alone with the silence and the light and the miles.

The road is paved all the way and only the last pitch is steep. There is ample level space on top for turning and parking.

RYAN was active as a borax town from 1914 to 1928, when operations shifted to Boron, near Mojave. A narrow-gauge railroad connected the six mines here and linked them to the Tonopah & Tidewater line, fifteen miles east at the edge of the Amargosa desert. The ore was colemanite, a form of borax named for William T. Coleman, the organizer of the first successful borax company in Death Valley. Buildings still stand at Ryan, but they are now sometimes used to house special groups and are consequently not open to the public. A 2-mile paved side road leads to Ryan.

GREENWATER boomed as a copper camp with a population of one thousand within a month of the first strike in 1905. It had a bank, a post office, telephones, a men's magazine, *The Chuckawalla*, a neighboring town called Furnace—everything except paying ore. Today all that remains are beer bottles, rusting stoves, pieces of Model T's, houseless basements, and dangerous vertical shafts, one of them 1,600 feet deep. Several abandoned roads lead to and through the townsites. Watch for the first one about 5 miles from the Dante's View road, on the Greenwater cutoff.

TOWNSITE REMNANTS

SALT CREEK

SALT CREEK AND THE SAND DUNES (Map 2)

Tour: SALT CREEK; the DEVIL'S CORNFIELD; the SAND DUNES, near Stove Pipe Wells Hotel (20 miles northwest of Furnace Creek).

Side Trip: STOVEPIPE WELL.

Suggested Time: Two or three hours; can be combined with a longer trip, such as Scotty's Castle or Rhyolite (see following tours, this chapter). Sunrise or sunset are ideal times in the Sand Dunes.

The turnoff to SALT CREEK is 2 miles north of the Daylight Pass road junction. Inch-long pupfish in the creek are holdovers from fish that swam in Lake Manly about 15,000 years ago. By tracing this genus of fish (*Cyprinodon,* species *salinus* here in Salt Creek) and also minnows of a different genus (*Siphateles*), geologists and ichthyologists have determined that Death Valley must once have been connected as far east as the Colorado River by a series of lakes. A short walk along the creek bank usually discloses the fish, swimming in schools. Watch also for killdeer and snipe, common among the grasses and rushes; and for the tracks of coyotes, ravens, and blue heron, which feed on the fish.

Northwest of Salt Creek is MC LEAN SPRING, where the Jayhawkers camped in 1849. In the 1930's a trading post operated near the spring, serving prospectors and adventurous tourists. It was a simple structure—a 10 × 20-foot canopy of marsh reed lashed together with wire from the old Rhyolite to Skidoo telephone line. The road to the spring is unmaintained.

The "corn shocks" of the DEVIL'S CORNFIELD are arrowweed bushes growing in peculiar clumps because of soil erosion. The plant's name comes from the Indians' use of its stalks for arrow shafts. On hot days the marsh of the Cornfield has the effect of a giant cooler, noticeably lowering the air temperature as its moisture evaporates from the surface of the ground.

SAND DUNES

Bare SAND DUNES cover fourteen square miles here, ever moving, but never getting anywhere. Wind ripples the surface and occasionally stirs up blinding sandstorms, but the main contours of the dunes are unchanged from year to year. Best access is from the Sand Dunes Campground, or from the unpaved Stovepipe Well road along the east edge of the Dunes.

Look in the sand for signs of the nighttime activity of wildlife: the footprints and tail marks of leaping kangaroo rats; the tracks of kitfox, perhaps including the dug-open remains of a hapless ground rodent's burrow; occasionally the talon marks and wing brushes of a hawk or owl that swooped down to capture dinner. The most delicate traceries of all belong to the *Eleodes* beetle ("stink bug"). Its feet make a row of tiny pinpricks on each side of the light line drawn by its dragging abdomen.

STOVEPIPE WELL, on the northeast fringe of the Dunes, was important enough as a waterhole on the old crossing of the valley that a small way station operated here during the days of Rhyolite and Skidoo. Only a historical marker identifies the site today. A rusted pump replaces the length of stovepipe originally sunk into the ground to keep the well open. (The hotel named for this well is ten miles southwest, on the main road.) The road to the well is unpaved but easily passable if one drives slowly; it is 3½ miles long, and connects between State 190 and the Scotty's Castle road.

DAYLIGHT PASS AND RHYOLITE (Map 2)

Tour: Up DAYLIGHT PASS to the ghost town of RHYOLITE (36 miles northeast of Furnace Creek).

Side Trips: SALT CREEK (see preceding tour); KEANE WONDER, CHLORIDE CLIFF, and TITUS CANYON, all on dirt roads (see following chapter).

Possible Loop Trip: On to BEATTY from Rhyolite, north on U.S. 95, and back into Death Valley via GRAPEVINE CANYON and SCOTTY'S CASTLE.

Suggested Time: Three or four hours to Rhyolite and back; all day with one or two of the side trips or the loop trip.

HELL'S GATE is 10 miles up the Daylight Pass road from its junction with State 190. Here teams en route from Rhyolite to Keane Wonder or Skidoo would toss their heads and snort as the heat of Death Valley struck them. "Must think they've stuck their noses into the gates of Hell!" a teamster remarked—and the name stuck.

Just beyond, a one-quarter-mile trail leads to HOLE IN THE ROCK SPRING, a small cave with a seep of fresh water that meant life for more than one wayfarer in the past. Listen to the "plink" of the water dropping into a small pool; and notice the tiny travertine stalagmites hanging from the ceiling.

Silence and empty shells of buildings in RHYOLITE do credit to the wisdom of Johnny Shoshone, a Death Valley Indian who traded his half of a mine that later produced a fortune for a few dollars and a pair of overalls. "White man come, make a big fuss, and go away," he used to say. "I still have my overalls."

From 1905 to 1908 Rhyolite was one of the most flourishing cities in Nevada. The ruins of the school, bank, doctor's office, and store still line Golden Street; the old jailhouse is on a side street. The Las Vegas & Tonopah Railroad depot and the Bottle House, built of 51,000 beer bottles, are open to the public with food and souvenirs for sale. The graveyard is a mile south of the Bottle House.

BULLFROG, site of the original strike, lies west of Rhyolite. The mine dumps prominent on the hill beyond it belonged to the Tramp Mine. On the opposite side of Rhyolite yawns the Glory Hole of the Montgomery-Shoshone Mine, a worthless hole now, but in its day the producer of ore rich enough to quarry, and abundant enough to keep an 18-stamp mill going full steam—for a while.

BOOTHILL CEMETERY, RHYOLITE

SCOTTY'S CASTLE AND UBEHEBE CRATER (Map 3)

Tour: To SCOTTY'S CASTLE and on to UBEHEBE CRATER (36 miles north of the Daylight Pass road junction).

Side Trips: SALT CREEK and the SAND DUNES (see detailed tour in this chapter); RACETRACK (see the following chapter on the back country).

Possible Loop Trip: Up GRAPEVINE CANYON to U.S. 95, south to BEATTY, and back to Death Valley via RHYOLITE.

Suggested Time: Five or six hours; more with side trips. Tours through the Castle are hourly during the travel season (make current inquiry).

DEATH VALLEY BUTTES lie east of the road close to the northern junction with the Daylight Pass road—gullied brown, buff, and brick-colored mud-hills backdropped by the dark rock of the Grapevine Mountains. Notice the Sand Dunes off to the west, rounded and soft-looking compared to the gullying and gouging close at hand.

SCOTTY'S CASTLE nestles among cottonwood trees near the mouth of Grapevine Canyon, a combination home and showplace. Two men thought Death Valley a fine place for a Moorish mansion with eighteen fireplaces and a 185-foot swimming pool; one of them had enough money to build it.

Walter Scott was a prospector and wild west show trick rider. Rumors of a gold mine surrounded his every move, and he had one—the pockets of Albert Johnson, a shy insurance millionaire from Chicago who took a fancy to the flamboyant desert rat from Death Valley. The two joined forces and with Scotty's enthusiasm and Johnson's wealth built the Castle, beginning in 1924.

Johnson died in 1948, Scotty in 1954, at the age of 81. A charitable foundation established by Johnson's will now operates the Castle, guiding visitors through for a nominal fee. Furnishings in the great halls and bedrooms are elaborate, many of them imported antiques and others made at the Castle by craftsmen who carefully modeled their work after Old World treasures. One entire room is devoted to an organ; water splashes over a jasper fountain into a fish pool in the living room; and wood for the fireplaces is stacked outside—120,000 railroad ties purchased when the Tonopah & Tidewater was torn up! Scotty is buried on top of a hill behind the "shack," as he loved to call the "castle" that Johnson built him.

UBEHEBE CRATER, a volcanic explosion pit, is 5 miles beyond the turnoff to the Castle. It measures a third of a mile across at the top and is eight hundred feet deep. It used to be a basket, the Indians say. They called it *Duh-vee'tah Wah'sah,* "Duhveetah's Carrying Basket." The name Ubehebe, sometimes mistranslated as "Basket in the Rock," actually was simply the name of a woman who lived near Duh-vee'tah Wah'sah.

Notice that Ubehebe is only one of half a dozen or more craters easily reached by walking south from the high point of Ubehebe's rim. (There is no trail.) Most are weathered to partial rims now. A nearly perfect volcanic cone rises within the remnant rim of one crater.

IN THE PANAMINTS (Map 4)

Tour: Through EMIGRANT CANYON, over to SKIDOO, on to AGUEREBERRY POINT (27½ miles from Stove Pipe Wells Hotel).

Side Trips: MOSAIC CANYON (see chapter on hiking); CHARCOAL KILNS; MAHOGANY FLAT.

Suggested Time: Half a day; longer with side trips. Aguereberry Point is best in afternoon light.

Brown cliffs with striking erosion patterns guard the entrance of EMIGRANT CANYON. They are fanglomerate—ancient alluvial fan material hardened into rock. HARRISBURG FLAT, at the head of the canyon, is an ancient

SCOTTY'S CASTLE

landscape, a remnant of the surface that existed before block faulting produced Death Valley. It is a senesland, a term derived from the Latin *senescere,* to grow old.

A 7-mile unpaved side road leads to the ghost town of SKIDOO. Notice the scar of the old water pipeline at right angles to the road, two miles after making the turn. During Skidoo's early days men hauled drinking water from Emigrant Spring and sold it for ten cents a gallon, but a better water source was needed before a mill could operate. Birch Spring, high on the side of Telescope Peak, seemed the only answer and men worked for over a year laying an eight-inch pipeline. This gave the town its water and its name, according to one story, for it was twenty-three miles to the spring, and "Twenty-three Skidoo" was the smart saying of the day. Other versions contend that twenty-three men founded the town; that two men made the original strike on the twenty-third of the month; that there were twenty-three important claims in the mining district.

Seven hundred people once lived in Skidoo. Today little is left except the graveyard and the silent tunnels and shafts which in their time were rich in gold—so rich that this town is unusual in Death Valley mining annals as actually having been profitable! Three million dollars went into the ground to develop the mines; six million came back out. One single stope yielded over one million dollars worth of ore. A fifteen-stamp mill processed the ore; the *Skidoo News* kept townsfolk up to date; the Tucki Consolidated Telephone & Telegraph linked them by wire to Rhyolite; mercantiles and saloons catered to needs; and in case of trouble a telegraph pole served as jail. Prisoners were handcuffed to it until arrangements were made for them at Independence, the county seat.

The Skidoo road usually is readily passable with care, but is not recommended for trailers. Below the townsite it climbs steadily, offering views of Death Valley and the Amargosa Desert. Notice Big Dune, rising beyond the Funeral Mountains; and Mount Charleston, a snow peak near Las Vegas.

A herd of goats, Skidoo's meat and milk supply, once grazed in the little flat between the Skidoo road and the Aguereberry Point road. Leaks in the Skidoo pipeline provided water, and grass sprouted among the sagebrush and saltbush.

AGUEREBERRY POINT takes its name from Pete Aguereberry, a Basque who came to herd sheep in Nevada but caught the gold fever. A few days before the Skidoo strike, in 1905, Pete Aguereberry and Shorty Harris found ore that quickly gave rise to HARRISBURG. In fact it was while lost on the way to Harrisburg that Harry Ramsey and One-Eye Thompson found the outcrop that started the Skidoo rush and a general bypassing of Harrisburg. It never was more than a tent city. Today it is a faint mark on the desert, discernible in the slanting light of a setting sun. Look for it south of the Aguereberry Point road, 1½ miles from its turn off the pavement.

CHARCOAL KILNS

Six thousand feet beneath Aguereberry Point, Death Valley stretches in plain view, from south of Badwater to Daylight Pass. Furnace Creek Wash shows as a wide, smooth pass between the Black Mountains and the Funerals; the hills behind the Inn shrink to mere wrinkles; and the Ranch is a square black patch joined to the Inn by the thread of its irrigation ditch. A short trail north from the parking area leads to the best overlook.

The 6½-mile road to the Point is unpaved and sometimes is washboarded. Two short canyons are fairly steep and winding, but pose no real difficulty. The road is not advised for trailers, however; and the road down Trail Canyon from Aguereberry Point is for jeeps only (extremely steep grades and sharp turns).

Ten CHARCOAL KILNS line a small canyon in upper Wildrose, on a side trip 8½ miles above Wild Rose Station. Swiss engineers designed them in the 1870's, Chinese laborers built them, and Indians cut pinyon pines to stoke them. Twenty-five miles west, in the mountains across Panamint Valley, the Modoc Mine needed charcoal for its smelter, and this was the nearest source of wood. The finished charcoal was packed to the mine on muleback. (The Modoc Mine was owned by George Hearst, father of the late William Randolph Hearst, the well-known publisher.)

The Kilns, thirty feet in diameter, are giant beehives of stone. A small lime kiln is up the hill behind them. Indians camped near here each fall to gather pinyon nuts, until about the time of World War II.

The road to the Kilns is steeper than it looks; driving in low gear may be advisable. Above the Kilns it definitely steepens, and in winter is often blocked by snow. No water is available above THORNDIKE's, a campground now, but the former home of an early-day prospector.

At MAHOGANY FLAT the road ends at 8,133 feet, the highest point in the Monument accessible by car. Walk along the Telescope Peak trail at least half a mile, to the first bench, and sit a while beneath the pines looking out across Death Valley. Something elemental whispers in a landscape so vast and empty, something soothing to the hard-pressed mind of modern man.

BACK COUNTRY ROAD, HARRISBURG FLAT

ARRASTRE

The Back Country by Car

Much of Death Valley's back country is accessible by dirt roads. These are easily passable for experienced and self-sufficient drivers but are perhaps best avoided by those accustomed only to pavement and readily available supplies and services. Road conditions vary; get current information at the National Park Service Visitor Center or a ranger station.

SARATOGA SPRINGS (Map 1)

Tour: South of ASHFORD MILL and CONFIDENCE MILL; across the AMARGOSA RIVER; past SHORELINE BUTTE, to SARATOGA SPRINGS (about 65 miles, either via Badwater or the West Side). Roads in the south end of the valley are irregularly maintained and seldom patrolled, but usually are readily passable; check current conditions.

Suggested Time: All day.

ASHFORD MILL, at the junction of the roads along the east and west sides of the valley, is a concrete monument to hope. It dates from a mining flurry during World War I. The Ashfords were three brothers who staked a claim up Scotty's Canyon, in the Black Mountains, then quickly sold it to a Hungarian nobleman for $60,000. He in turn sold it for $105,000, and the new owners naïvely built a fifty-ton mill out in the floor of the valley and waited for a fortune that never came. They built the mill's walls heavy enough for a fortress—but only because the freight company delivered one carload of cement more than they had ordered, and shipping it back would have been too costly!

The CONFIDENCE MILL site (7 miles south) processed gold from a mine that may first have been worked by Mexicans before 1849. Crude ore-crushing mills (*arrastres*) and reduction furnaces found at several points in Death Valley point to their early arrival here. The '49ers found one of the furnaces when they first entered Death Valley; hence the name Furnace Creek. Such evidence of Mexican miners is widespread in the Mojave but difficult to date, because the men clung to outmoded equipment that could make a mine seem very old when in reality it was simply worked by very old methods.

Notice the AMARGOSA RIVER, crossed by the road 4 miles south of Confidence Mill. It is a remnant watercourse, still bringing water into Death Valley as it did during the Ice Age days of Lake Manly. SHORELINE BUTTE, a black hill of basalt thrusting up from the valley floor southwest of here, shows terraces washed into its flanks by successive levels of the lake.

SARATOGA SPRINGS (17 miles south of Confidence Mill) is at the extreme south end of Death Valley—a place to camp a day or two and explore. Three large ponds are "home" for waterbirds in winter (especially for coots), and for pupfish the year around. These pupfish are *Cyprinodon nevadensis nevadensis,* a different subspecies from the C. *nevadensis amargosae* that swim in the Amargosa River or the C. *salinus* in Salt Creek. Hills of black stone dotted with silvery desert holly drop from the mountains to the valley floor, their toes awash in the ponds and fringed with reeds six feet high.

Beside the main spring (no swimming) is a crude stone cabin and an athel tree big enough to shade fifty people. Behind, in the Ibex Mountains, roads lead to mines, but most of them are advisable only for trucks or jeeps and experienced drivers. To the south, high dunes pile against the base of the mountains.

Saratoga is a place to be alone, to hear the silence and to watch light move across the land, changing the contours and the moods.

KEANE WONDER AND CHLORIDE CLIFF (Map 2)

Tour: KEANE WONDER and KEANE SPRING at the base of the Funeral Mountains; CHLORIDE CITY and CHLORIDE CLIFF at the top (22 miles north of Furnace Creek to Keane Wonder; 43 miles to Chloride Cliff). Check current road conditions.

The road to KEANE WONDER turns off the southern Daylight Pass approach road 6 miles from its junction with State 190. From the turnoff the road dips and climbs across the fan for 4 miles, and is usually passable if driven slowly.

Gold was found at Keane Wonder in 1903, two years before the more spectacular Bulldog strike gave rise to Rhyolite. The ore was rich enough so that by 1907 a twenty-stamp mill was crushing 1,800 tons of it per month. Only the foundation of the mill and the rusting bullwheel remain; the timbers were salvaged in 1954, part of the desert tradition of building a new camp from the material left at an old one. The mine is about one mile up the mountainside from the mill (see the chapter on hikes).

Walk north along the old road as far as the mineral springs (about half a mile) to see travertine terraces and spillways and pools made colorful by algae. Beyond is the old house where the superintendent of the Keane Extension Mine once lived—evidently with his family, for scraps of toys lie among the usual camp litter of discarded shoes, magazines, and sardine cans. (Beware unmarked vertical shafts.)

Eight miles up the Daylight Pass highway from the Keane Wonder Mill Road is the turn to KEANE SPRING (2½-mile road). This was the water source for Chloride City, on the crest of the Funerals. A pump lifted water the 3,500 feet and a patrolman walked the pipeline, guarding against leaks. The old road from the pumphouse to Chloride City is washed out now and impassable even by jeep.

CHLORIDE CITY boomed twice: first from 1878 to 1883, and again from 1905 to 1910, during Rhyolite's heyday. (Several roads approach Chloride City from the Nevada side of the mountains. Abrupt cross-washes often make them rough; ask which is currently the best.) Several frame houses stand empty to the wind in the old city and its "suburbs." Three houses are dug part way into the bank of a wash, and walled the rest of the way— a typical desert style called "Cousin Jack," after the Welsh miners who brought the technique from the old country.

Park a mile beyond Chloride City (steep grade) and walk the last one thousand feet to CHLORIDE CLIFF. Death Valley unfolds directly below: Tucki Mountain and the Sand Dunes, due west; the white shimmer of the salt flats, to the south; the almost equally white beds of ancient Lake Rogers, to the north.

"COUSIN JACK," CHLORIDE CITY

TITUS CANYON (Map 2)

Tour: Up Daylight Pass, then through TITUS CANYON past the ghost town of LEADFIELD and KLARE SPRING (about 60 miles northwest of Furnace Creek to the narrows of lower Titus Canyon).

Suggested Time: All day.

The TITUS CANYON road turns off the Beatty Highway 7 miles east of the California-Nevada state line. Ask about current conditions before starting. The road is closed from mid-May to mid-October because of cloudburst danger. The trip is recommended only for experienced rough-road drivers.

The canyon name commemorates Morris Titus, a Rhyolite miner who set out with two partners on a prospecting trip. For two days they found

MOUTH OF TITUS CANYON

nothing but dry springs, so with only twenty gallons of water left for three men and twenty-one head of stock, Titus decided to push ahead to a spring in Death Valley. He never returned. The only trace of him was found later by a survey party out of Goldfield. Reminiscing about it, S. G. Benedict wrote: "When the chief and I were riding up a canyon . . . we came upon his [Titus's] last message to his partners—'Have gone down the canyon looking for the spring. Have been waiting for you. Titus.' "

For its first 12 miles the Titus Canyon road crosses the Amargosa Desert and winds up the Grapevine Mountains to BLOODY GAP. Directly below is LEADFIELD, a mine flurry stirred up in 1925 by C. C. Julian, one of Death Valley's most successful promoters. He blasted some tunnels and salted the dumps with lead ore brought from Tonopah; then he distributed handbills showing ships steaming up the Amargosa River to Titus Canyon and loading ore. With this he lured investors! Three or four buildings still stand and piles of weathered lumber mark the collapse of others.

KLARE SPRING, 2½ miles below the town, was the main water supply. Here dusty miners once doused themselves for "50¢ a Shower" with water from a fifty-gallon drum mounted on a rickety platform. Notice the petroglyphs chipped into the rock behind the spring—"Indian writing" of unknown age and meaning.

The NARROWS twist between limestone walls that are five hundred feet sheer and only fifteen to fifty feet apart. Two miles below Klare Spring notice the water ripple marks corrugating the rock of the south wall—marks made when this rock was silt in a stream bed or lake bottom. About three miles farther the canyon walls are breccia, a natural mosaic of black, gray, and white. On the outsides of the curves, look for walls hollowed and polished by the water and gravel that churns down the canyon after a cloudburst. Watch too for the great mounds of loose rock that spill from high on the rim. (One of the most spectacular is just above Klare Spring, on the south side of the canyon.)

Six miles below Klare Spring the canyon rounds a last bend and bursts upon a view of Tin Mountain and northern Death Valley. Three miles down the fan is the Scotty's Castle highway. Look back from it and try to see Titus Canyon, a slot so narrow it scarcely shows.

THE RACETRACK (Map 3)

Tour: Beyond Ubehebe Crater to the RACETRACK with its MOVING ROCKS; a side trip to HIDDEN VALLEY and GOLDBELT for the adventurous (31 miles southwest of Scotty's Castle to the Racetrack).

Suggested Time: All day.

Prepare for disappointment as far as the Moving Rocks are concerned; little evidence remains. However, the drive is scenic and the road usually good.

MOVING
ROCKS

Edging south out of the black cinders of Ubehebe Crater, the road leads between the Cottonwood and Last Chance ranges and through one of the best stands of cactus in Death Valley. Cottontop, cholla, beavertail, and hedgehog are profuse. Farther on, Joshua trees speckle Tin Mountain up to the beginning of the pinyon-juniper belt.

Twenty miles from the pavement at Ubehebe is TEAKETTLE JUNCTION: take the right-hand fork to the Racetrack (6 miles) and the left-hand fork to Hidden Valley (10 miles). For years a teakettle lay forlornly beneath a creosote bush here, the only distinguishing feature of this road junction. "Turn right at the old teakettle and keep straight as far as the rocking chair . . ." is typical of early-day directions. Or sometimes graves were used: "Go south to Tim Ryan, then turn left," and so forth.

The RACETRACK is named, probably without basis, for Indian horse races that were supposedly run on the smooth oval of the dry lake with spectators watching from the "island" near the north end, the Grandstand. MOVING ROCKS were mentioned as early as the 1900's by prospectors, but they were not studied by geologists until the 1950's. Today, few are left in place and time and tire tracks have almost erased their traces. (Try the strongly slanting light of sunup or sundown for the best chance of finding tracks.)

The largest rocks, weighing from 200 to 600 pounds, were blocks of limestone near the south end of the lake. One of these had furrowed a track 220 feet long into the mud of the playa. Longer tracks, made by smaller rocks, measured up to 800 feet long and included right-angle jogs and complete loops. Geologists do not agree on precisely how the rocks moved, although no one disputes the fact they did move, and did so naturally. Similar tracks are found on other playas, including Bonnie Claire in the Grapevine Mountains (no longer visible).

Wind is the most probable explanation. Laboratory experiments indicate that a gust of wind 100 miles per hour would be enough to move most of the rocks if the playa was wet to a depth of three or four centimeters. (The surface is exceedingly slippery when wet, but in mud deeper than four centimeters the rocks sink enough to greatly increase the force needed to move them.) Ice may have been a factor along with wind; part of the weight of the rocks may have been supported by ice collars or floes.

HIDDEN VALLEY lies beyond Lost Burro Gap. It is a valley nestled high in the Cottonwood Mountains, much like the Racetrack. One side road climbs to an abandoned asbestos mine on the mountain crest overlooking Death Valley; another leads to the Lost Burro Mine. The main road goes beyond Hidden Valley, crosses ULIDA FLAT, and reaches GOLDBELT, an area of intermittent mining. Many of these roads are passable in a car, but make advance inquiry and explore them gingerly. Solitude is almost assured here— a blessing to those who seek it, but a grave inconvenience to those who venture beyond their driving experience and find themselves in difficulty.

WEST SIDE SPRINGS AND BUTTE VALLEY (Map 4)

Tour: Across the DEVIL'S GOLFCOURSE; along the WEST SIDE SPRINGS and WELLS; past the HANAUPAH FAULT SCARP and the HARRIS-DAYTON GRAVES to EAGLE BORAX WORKS; up WARM SPRINGS CANYON to BUTTE VALLEY (63 miles southwest of Furnace Creek). West Side road is unpaved but maintained and usually very good; Butte Valley road varies.

Suggested Time: Two or three hours to go as far as Eagle Borax Works and return; all day for Butte Valley.

The salt of the DEVIL'S GOLFCOURSE begins 1½ miles after turning off the Badwater road. The pinnacles here are not so high or so white as those near the Salt Pools, but the landscape is equally bleak. (The entire area of salt flats is called the Devil's Golfcourse. It is accessible by road at two separate points: here, and at the Salt Pools north of Badwater.)

TULE SPRING (5 miles south of the Devil's Golfcourse) is where the stricken Bennett and Arcane families probably camped in 1849, awaiting

STRIPED BUTTE

return of the two young men scouting ahead to find the settlements. However, present-day Indians recall their grandparents telling of the "hairy-faced ones" staying at *Toah Poize*, Bennett's Well, thereby keeping the Shoshones out of a winter camp that they prized highly because of its fine mesquite and good water.

Notice the HANAUPAH FAULT SCARP west of Tule Spring, a ten- to thirty-foot embankment paralleling the foot of the Panamint Mountains, part of the block faulting that dropped the floor of Death Valley. For years this fault and others were thought to have occurred in the late 1800's, during a period of great earthquakes. But the recent discovery of Indian storage pits dug into the debris of the fault scarps disproves the date, for the Indian material is much older than the late nineteenth century.

The HARRIS-DAYTON GRAVES (1½ miles farther south) belong to the "mine fever" days. Jim Dayton was a caretaker at Furnace Creek Ranch who died in the summer of 1899, while on a trip out to get supplies. Dolph Nevares and Frank Tilton, co-workers of Dayton's, found his body lying in the shade of a mesquite, his dog faithfully on guard alongside. "Well, Jimmy, you lived in the heat and died in the heat, and now I suppose you've gone to hell," Tilton murmured in eulogy as he and Nevares dug a grave.

Shorty Harris died in 1934. His request had been, "Bury me beside Jim Dayton in the valley we love. Above me write: 'Here lies Shorty Harris, a single-blanket jackass prospector.'"

The site of EAGLE BORAX WORKS, first borax plant in Death Valley, is off the road to the east, 3 miles south of Tule Spring. A man named Isidore Daunet found borax here in 1875 as he was heading for Arizona from Panamint City; but he gave it no thought until six years later when the excitement of Aaron Winters's discovery at Furnace Creek spread across the desert. In 1881 Daunet came back, located a two-hundred-sixty-acre claim, bought an iron vat and six one-thousand-gallon pans in Daggett, and freighted them the one hundred forty miles to Death Valley. He hired fifty men and began refining borax. It proved impure and the best price Daunet could get was eight cents per pound, one quarter of the standard price. Operations soon ceased.

All that remains are the scars left by the crystallizing pans and furrows scraped into the marsh to facilitate the leaching of borax. The trees here are athels, native to Africa but thoroughly naturalized in the American desert. Ponds usually form in winter, making this a fine place to watch for both songbirds and waterbirds.

Two roads lead up the fan to WARM SPRING CANYON. The southernmost one, 19½ miles south of Eagle Borax Works, is the better maintained. Notice the bands of white striping the brown hills. This is talc. At Warm Spring miners are tunneling a vein of talc twenty-five feet thick and three-quarters of a mile long, most of it steatite, the purest talc, which is used in over one hundred industries. For nineteen years, while the claims were being developed, one of the owners supported the mine with poker winnings, which were said to total $40,000. In recent years the wife of the mine's manager had worked her way through college by dealing faro!

The mine is not open to the public, but notice the huge oleander bushes and fig trees shading the cookhouse and bunkhouse, examples of what water can do in the desert. The fig trees were planted about 1900.

BUTTE VALLEY lies 3 miles farther, a broad plain at 4,500 feet elevation. STRIPED BUTTE rises from the level floor, an abrupt, calico-banded peak that intrigues geologists because it is plainly sedimentary, although the surrounding country is granite.

Roads and wheel tracks in Butte Valley fork off every few miles, usually ending at abandoned mines. Sample them cautiously and with a sense of impending discovery: Anvil Spring is distinguished by a lone cottonwood tree and a stone cabin once used by a geologist and known as the Geologist's Shack ever since. Above it is Greater View Spring, once the home of Carl Mengel, a prospecting partner of Shorty Harris, and now the location of his grave.

REDLANDS CANYON, believed by historians to be the way the Bennett-Arcane party may have left Death Valley in 1849, is nearby (but passable only part way, in a jeep). A three-stamp gold mill stands in a small granite amphitheater. It was built by Mengel in 1898, reputedly with timbers salvaged from the construction of the old Third Street tunnel in Los Angeles and hauled up Goler Wash by mules to the mill site.

On a separate set of tracks, beyond the mill, is a prospector's "house"—walled up beneath the overhang of a boulder the size of a railroad car—a simple shelter with one front wall, the hillside for the other three, and the boulder for roof. Above it is Outlaw Cave, a small dark hole where a stolen Wells Fargo safe once was found, blasted open and quite empty.

TRAIL CANYON

Trips by Truck and Jeep

Many old mine roads impassable by car are readily passable in a truck or jeep. These have few directional signs and are not maintained or patrolled; some are mere sets of tracks. Ask about current conditions, then navigate by topographic maps (available at the National Park Service Visitor Center or by mail from the Death Valley Natural History Association).

Regulations now prohibit driving off established roadways, for while solitude still lingers up the canyons there are many who seek it—and increasing numbers inevitably mean increasing regulations, a basic principle underlying society. Random driving breaks bushes and scars the landscape with wheel tracks, destroying the pristine quality which the National Monument is established to protect and pass on intact to future generations.

BLACK MOUNTAINS (Map 1)

Greenwater Canyon: The road turns north off the Greenwater cutoff, 8½ miles beyond the Dante's View pavement. It soon enters a wash that is both steep and sandy, making this approach advisable only by jeep, although trucks usually can come in from the other end of the road for 10 miles or more.

Watch along the canyon walls for Indian petroglyphs, and for pictographs on the ceilings of caves in a side canyon about 3½ miles from the Greenwater end of the road. They are drawn in red and black, and depict deer, bighorn sheep, and men dancing and riding horseback. (Pictographs, *painted on* rock, are rare in Death Valley; petroglyphs, *pecked into* the rock, are frequent.) The Lila C Mine and the site of the first town of Ryan are small marks on the desert at the eastern edge of the hills (9 miles from the Greenwater road). Notice the bed of the Tonopah & Tidewater Railroad, first built as a spur north from the mainline at Baker to haul Lila C borax, and later pushed on to the gold boomtowns of Rhyolite and Goldfield. In 1913 mining operations switched from this Ryan to the "new" Ryan nearer Death Valley.

Gold Valley: Mines operated in this mountain-rimmed basin during the Greenwater boom. (The road, usually passable in a truck, turns off the

Greenwater road 13 miles from the paved road to Dante's View.) An old mill stands at the headwaters of Willow Creek, about 4 miles beyond Gold Valley itself. Water usually is sufficient to flow along the creek bed and over a seventy-five-foot cascade into the head reaches of Willow Spring Canyon, a gorge plunging directly down the flanks of the Black Mountains into Death Valley.

Others: Ibex Mountains behind Saratoga Springs; a maze of roads, most of them passable in a truck. *Funeral Peak*, with a hike to the summit. *Deadman's Pass*, to loop back to Death Valley Junction. *Montgomery Pass*, jeeps only, for a sweeping view of Death Valley before dropping into Rhodes Wash. *Ash Meadows*, flat country east of Death Valley Junction with roads past ranches and warm springs (including *Devil's Hole*, one of the four locations of "desert sardines," *Cyprinodons*).

FUNERAL MOUNTAINS (Map 2)

Echo Canyon: The tracks up Echo Canyon turn toward the Funerals 2 miles east of Furnace Creek Inn. Loose gravel often makes it impassable except in a jeep or a truck with compound low gear. Notice the ten-foot "window" in the south wall of the canyon, just inside the mouth (5 miles from the highway). Keep right at the fork, 2 miles farther, for Schwaub, which boomed in 1905 and stirred again twenty years later as the Inyo

NEEDLE'S EYE,
ECHO CANYON

NITER BEDS

Mine Company. Most of the houses still standing belong to the later date. Beyond the camp watch for an anticline, an upside-down "U" in the rock strata (on the north side of wash) and for Indian petroglyphs (on the south side).

The left-hand fork of the central canyon leads to a maze of roads and a succession of deserted mine camps. It ends at a saddle near Nevares Peak, which offers a view up Death Valley to the north end.

Others: South from Chloride Cliff along the crest of the Funerals to *Gold Dollar Mine* and *Indian Pass*; jeeps only. South from Beatty roughly along the old T & T route to *Big Dune* and to *Leeland* and other old camps and stations; level country, usually possible in a truck.

GRAPEVINE MOUNTAINS (Map 2)

Wahguyhe Peak: A truck can get about as far as the ridge; a jeep is needed to drop over into Fall Canyon. The road turns off the pavement 11 miles north of Beatty, heading toward the first canyon north of Wahguyhe Peak. It climbs among steel-blue boulders, crosses the bed of the old Rhyolite railway, and is joined by various north–south mine roads dating from the glory days of the 1900's. From the crest of the range the view is of north Death Valley framed by pinyon pines. Indians used to camp here to gather nuts and to hunt deer and bighorn sheep.

VALLEY FLOOR (Map 3)

Mesquite Flat and Niter Beds: Approach from the old road heading north of Stove Pipe Wells Hotel service station, or from Midway Well on the

Scotty's Castle road. Road condition depends on cross-cutting washes and the amount of loose sand; it is sometimes passable in a truck, sometimes only in a jeep. The area is a jumble of mesquite hummocks used through the centuries as campsites by the Indians. (Collecting or excavating is forbidden.) A few poles of the old Rhyolite–Skidoo telephone line still stand and insulators lie buried in the sand. The Niter Beds are strange undulating white clay beds on the northwest edge of Mesquite Flat, a remnant of Pleistocene Lake Rogers. The last distance to the beds themselves must be covered on foot.

COTTONWOOD MOUNTAINS (Map 3)

Lemoigne Canyon: Jean Lemoigne was a French engineer brought to America in 1881 by Isidore Daunet to supervise the Eagle Borax Works, then starting in southern Death Valley. But before he arrived, the illfated venture had failed and Daunet had committed suicide. Lemoigne stayed on to prospect.

The tracks to the canyon turn off the highway 3 miles below the Emigrant Ranger Station. They cross the fan, enter the Lemoigne Wash after 5 miles, and end at a mine 4½ miles later. Passable only by jeep.

Cottonwood Canyon: Turn up the Cottonwood Fan west of the Stove Pipe Wells Hotel service station. The route often is difficult to find; watch for cairns (some topped with white stones, an Indian system of marking a route that led to water). The road ends about 10 miles beyond the narrows of the canyon, but be sure to stroll farther along the cottonwood-shaded stream—a rare opportunity in the supposedly arid wastes of Death Valley. Usually the canyon is accessible only in a jeep, although sometimes compound low gear is enough.

Marble Canyon: Watch for tracks branching north from lower Cottonwood Canyon. Drive to the narrows, then walk. Black limestone walls rise sheer, well polished by water. In places they are only ten to fifteen feet apart. Watch for petroglyphs, which are frequent, and for a single inscription of the date "1849" and nearby initials "J.B." chipped into the south wall a quarter of a mile beyond the second narrows. This is evidence that the Pinney-Savage split of the Jayhawker Party left Death Valley by this canyon. A man named Baker was in the group, and he could have been the "J.B."

Hunter Mountain and Saline Valley: Several jeep and truck roads penetrate the Cottonwood Mountains south of the Racetrack, all of them with frequent pine- and juniper-framed views, old mine camps, and springs where bighorn sheep and wild burros water. Only one route leads out of Death Valley National Monument into Saline Valley, dropping down Jackass Canyon from Hunter Mountain. A salt mine operated in Saline Valley beginning in 1913. The company built a tramway thirteen and a half miles

MARBLE CANYON

over the mountains to Owens Lake; it was one of the longest trams in the world in its day, and unquestionably crossed some of the most rugged terrain. Three hundred buckets swung from the cables, delivering twenty tons an hour to the terminal. The mine operated intermittently until the 1930's, when depletion of the best salt deposits plus the general financial panic conspired to close it.

TUCKI MOUNTAIN (Map 3)

Telephone Canyon: Jeep only. Turn off the pavement 2 miles up Emigrant Wash from the Ranger Station; half a mile later turn right up the cut in the bank; 2½ miles farther turn right into a side canyon; walk to an arch bridging from wall to wall. The main road winds and climbs 8 or 10 miles farther to a mine.

Grotto Canyon: See the chapter on hiking.

PANAMINT MOUNTAINS (Map 4)

Trail Canyon: The road drops from Aguereberry Point with steep grades and one switchback sharp enough to require backing. (It is a one-way road, downhill only; be sure brakes are good. Ask about current condition; often washed out.)

Roads 4 miles below the Point branch to mines. The middle fork road ends in 2 miles at a dam, near an abandoned camp. The south fork road ends in 2½ miles at a tramway leading to the old Morning Glory Mine tunnel. The ore is a beautiful mottle of gray, blue, and green—a complex of lead, silver, and zinc. Trail Canyon was the one the Indians climbed each summer, moving from the valley heat into the coolness of the mountains.

Hanaupah Canyon: The road is usually passable in a truck, but is for skilled rough-road drivers only; watch for loose gravel in the upper wash. The road turns off the West Side road 2 miles north of Eagle Borax Works, then cuts through the Hanaupah Fault Scarp and up the fan. Near the mouth of the canyon it drops to the floor of the wash, which is about seventy-five feet deep at this point. The slope is less steep than it appears and will not pose an undue problem on the way back up. (The wash floor slopes at an opposite angle from the road, creating an optical illusion.) The road ends at a mine camp and a tangle of willows. Above it a spring bubbles from the hillside and watercress usually patches the dusty brown slope with emerald green. The canyon forks here: the southern draw leads to a series of cascades and pools; the northern to a twenty-five-foot waterfall. Notice the fine view of Telescope Peak and the surrounding high Panamints—or sample it directly by hiking from the ridge north of the mine. Better yet, arrange transportation and hike downhill to a waiting car.

Wingate Pass: In the 1880's twenty-mule teams climbed out of Death Valley over this pass. Drivers dubbed it "Windy Gap" because a wind always seemed to be stirring up dust, tormenting teams and men. Through the years this became Wind Gate, and ultimately the *d* was dropped, making it Wingate. In the 1920's fate dealt cruelly with the backers of an Epsom salt mine near the summit. They had a monorail built from the railroad at Trona to the mine at Epsomite, but the first engine proved too weak to pull the cars and the second was so heavy that it sank the A-frames of the monorail into the mire of Searles Lake!

The west side of Wingate Pass is outside of Death Valley National Monument on Naval Ordnance Test Station land; it is closed to public travel without special permission. On the east side, the road up Wingate turns toward the Panamints 6 miles north of Ashford Junction.

Johnson Canyon: See the chapter on hiking.

Panamint City: Here was a wild camp—fifty fatal shootings in the four years that the town boomed! Wells Fargo took one look and refused to handle Panamint City bullion, an extraordinary action on their part, but one that merely teased the ingenuity of Panamint City men. They shipped the silver down Surprise Canyon and across the desert to the railroad in open freight wagons without so much as an armed guard. But they first cast it into quarter-ton balls—too heavy for the local highwaymen to gallop off with!

The brick smokestack of the old mill towers alone today. The only other remnants of the 1874 to 1878 boom are a few stone walls. (The frame buildings are from a subsequent flurry in the 1920's.) The road turns off the old, unpaved Panamint Valley road 1 mile north of Ballarat. From there to Panamint City is 9 miles, usually passable in a truck. Notice the arrastre (crude gold mill) 1 mile after turning up the fan.

Others: Up *Pleasant Canyon* past the site of Radcliff, where a twenty-stamp mill operated in 1898 and a Chinese cook sent dinner up the tramway to men in the mine; along the crest of the Panamints; and down *South Park Canyon* through spectacular narrows.

PANAMINT CITY

Where to Hike

Bare slopes, dry washes, and narrow canyons invite exploration on foot, and serve as natural trails. The openness of the desert simplifies finding the way, and topographic maps provide detailed information on distances and landmarks. Be sure to let someone know before starting out, and to check back in with them upon returning. Never hike alone. Do carry water.

Ideally, many hikes can be one way. Part of a party can hike and the rest can drive to a prearranged pick-up point. Or two carloads can park at opposite ends of a hike, then meet midway on the trail and exchange car keys.

VALLEY FLOOR

Salt Flats (Map 1): Hike from Badwater to Eagle Borax Works, or the other way. The salt formations are surprisingly varied: pinnacles and paper-thin cupolas; great "saucers" six feet across, bounded by pressure ridges and frosted with salt crystals; expanses as smooth as a billiard table; hummocks that drum underfoot. Small streams meander short distances. A well-built roadway raised five feet above the salt runs east–west for perhaps a tenth of a mile and then stops as abruptly and mysteriously as it began. There is no particular trail; pick the best route—and prepare to sink ankle-deep in briny ooze at times. Allow half a day.

Golden Canyon (Map 1): Established trails lead from the end of the road to Red Cathedral and to Manly Beacon. These are half-hour hikes. For slightly longer, hike through to Zabriskie Point past Manly Beacon.

Haystacks (Map 2): Park at Harmony Borax Works and walk northwest to the checkerboard mounds of borax out in the valley. Borax Company men mounded the marsh mud this way in the 1880's to increase the formation of cottonball borax, which leached out into the hollows between the mounds. The name Haystacks comes from the slight resemblance to a field of hay newly mowed and raked into windrows. The way usually is muddy, with a flowing small stream to cross. An hour or two each way suffices.

Salt Creek (Map 2): Here is a below-sea-level hike, along a flowing creek, in Death Valley! Watching for fish in the eddies is only the begin-

RED CATHEDRAL

ning of interests. Keep an eye out for cinnamon teal and snipes and herons —and for coyotes, which occasionally add a side dish of waterfowl to their standard diet of rodents and mesquite beans. Their tracks can usually be found in the mud, even when the animals themselves are not seen. Notice too the variety of plants growing in this saline soil: salt grass, several salt-bushes, pickleweed. The hills bordering the creek are a study in erosion patterns, and from their crests they offer good views of Daylight Pass and Death Valley Buttes to the north, and of Telescope Peak to the south. Plan on anywhere from half an hour to all day.

Sand Dunes (Map 2): A particular delight at sunrise and sunset, or in the moonlight. A sure favorite with barefooted children. Watch for animal holes and tracks as well as the ripples etched by the wind.

Ubehebe Crater (Map 3): Climb to the high point of Ubehebe's rim and walk south among the series of remnant craters at least as far as Little Hebe, a perfect new crater within the broken rim of an old one. Geologists think it may be only about one thousand years old—exceedingly recent on the geologic time scale. Plan to spend from one hour to half a day.

BLACK MOUNTAINS

Dante's View (Map 1): To sense the primordial mood of Death Valley and the ruggedness of its terrain, walk north from the Dante's View parking area along the mountain crest. An easy hike—for ten minutes, or an hour.

Willow Springs (Map 1): The approach road is rough, but usually passable in a truck or a car with high clearance; check current conditions. From the end of the road, walk down canyon a half-mile or more, following a stream that drops through a series of pools. Watch for wildlife, including bighorn sheep.

LITTLE HEBE CRATER

TRAMWAY, KEANE WONDER

FUNERAL MOUNTAINS

Keane Wonder (Map 2): A good trail leads from the mill site up the tramway to the Keane Wonder Mine (about 1 mile, but steep in places). The bunkhouses still stand, now the domain of pack rats. The tunnels of this mine are more dangerous than most. The ceilings of great vaults are unsupported, and walls and floors are pocked by unexpected stopes and chutes. Time and transportation permitting, the hike can be continued to Chloride City at the top of the mountains. Or drive to Chloride and walk down the old road to Keane Spring, a different route from the one from mill to mine. (Keane Spring is toward Daylight Pass from the mill, on a separate side road.)

Other hikes are north along the fault line at the base of the mountains, past mineral springs and prospect holes; or drive to the first canyon mouth south of the mill and walk up the wash through the narrows. Time depends on distances undertaken.

MOSAIC CANYON

GROTTO CANYON

TUCKI MOUNTAIN

Mosaic Canyon (Map 3): Reached by a graded road that turns toward Tucki Mountain from near Stove Pipe Wells Hotel. The hike can be short or long depending on time and energy: walk half a mile up the wash, sampling the canyon; or persevere to its head, about 9 miles. Water-polished breccia patterns the walls of the lower canyon with a natural mosaic of white, gray, and black rock. Watch also for white marble. Much of the canyon floor is marble, but the amount currently showing depends on whether the last cloudburst covered it over with gravel and mud or washed it clean.

Grotto Canyon (Map 3): Usually approachable only by jeep because of washouts and gravel (the turnoff is 2½ miles east of Stove Pipe Wells Hotel). The first grotto is about a half mile from the canyon mouth, but continue beyond. Water-carved grottoes follow close upon each other in succession, their walls hollowed and polished, and in places almost meeting overhead. The way becomes a challenge, for increasingly high dry waterfalls must be scaled. How high they are depends on how much gravel the last runoff washed over their rims and mounded against their bases. Allow half a day, or longer.

PANAMINT MOUNTAINS

Telescope Peak (Map 4): Here January hikers have found twelve-foot cornices of snow and May hikers have been closed in by blizzard and fog. The trail leads through pine trees (pinyons, limber pines, and bristlecones) and across Arcane Meadow, then climbs above timberline to the summit. There are magnificent views from the Charleston Mountains in the east to the Sierra Nevada in the west. Telescope Peak was named in 1860 by W. T. Henderson, the first man to climb it. "You can see so far it's just like looking through a telescope!" he exclaimed, with more fervor than logic.

The trail, 7½ miles one way, is a long day's hike or is ideal as an overnight between April and November, depending on snow conditions. Carry water. Snow equipment is needed in winter; check in at Wildrose Ranger Station.

Skidoo Pipeline (Map 4): The old pipe from Birch Spring to Skidoo (23 miles) is in place part of the way and its scar is plain most of the rest of the way. The pipe had hardly begun to deliver water in 1906 before a dispute arose between the builders and the lessees, which ended with the builders tearing out one section. But the lessees cared little. The Skidoo boom was about to bust anyway.

There is no trail, and much rough going. Hike the whole way, or segments. From upper Wildrose Canyon, where the pipeline crosses the road, or to Birch Spring, high on Telescope Peak, is probably the most interesting portion. There is a good chance of seeing wild burros.

Hungry Bill's Ranch (Map 4): "Vegetables of all kinds are much needed and would command a good figure. We paid $2.40 for two heads of cabbage last week," announced the *Panamint City News* on February 27, 1875. To fill the need, some enterprising men from Switzerland set out a fruit and nut orchard in upper Johnson Canyon, ten miles from Panamint City over the crest of the mountains. They also planted vegetables and boarded horses "on reasonable terms." The fields and corrals still pattern the canyon bottom, and a few rusting horseshoes, a horse collar, and a plow lie discarded among the black walnuts fallen from the trees. Hungry Bill was a Shoshone Indian whose family traditionally camped in Johnson Canyon each summer. He filed homestead papers on the ranch after the Swiss left so as to protect his ancestral ownership rights.

Experienced desert drivers usually can cajole a truck up the fan almost to the mouth of Johnson Canyon, although in some years loose gravel makes it necessary to stop lower down. The ranch is up the main draw of the north fork; no trail or signs, but little problem of direction. Watch for three arrastres (crude ore-crushing mills) in the floor of the canyon and the flume that carried water to one of them. If possible, hike beyond the ranch, over Sentinel Gap to Panamint City (about 10 miles one way)—the old "fresh vegetable" route.

The south fork of Johnson Canyon has several springs and abandoned mines—plus many fine views. Plan on a long day for each fork.

FURNACE CREEK WASH

Directory

ENTRANCE ROADS

Plan to enter Death Valley by one road and leave by another. Check the chapters on sights to see along main roads and back country roads, to be sure not to miss points of interest while entering or leaving. Remember that the miles are long between sources of gasoline, water, and help; be sure that supplies are ample before starting out. Tanks of water for refilling radiators are located every few miles on the main entrance roads as supplements to springs and settlements. Some of the unpaved roads are closed in summer because of washouts or other hazards.

PAVED ROADS

Wildrose Canyon–Emigrant Pass: Scenic route from Los Angeles, allowing a sample of the canyons and flats typical of the Panamint Mountains. One steep, narrow, winding section of road (Rattlesnake Canyon, above Wild Rose Station) is likely to be difficult for large trailers.

Towne's Pass: Route of the Eichbaum Toll Road, first automobile road into Death Valley, opened in 1926. Steep, and looks it, on the west side; steep, and doesn't look it, on the east side: use low driving ranges to avoid burning out brakes. A quick entrance from the west, but with less of interest along the way than via Wildrose Canyon and Emigrant Pass.

Grapevine Canyon: A route from the north with entry through a canyon, past Scotty's Castle, and down the entire length of Death Valley.

Daylight Pass: Main route from Reno, with striking view of the Valley from Hell's Gate, the pass between the Grapevine and Funeral mountains. Watch for wildflowers in spring.

Furnace Creek Wash: Route by which the pioneers entered in 1849. Easy grades; main entrance from Las Vegas. Scenic in itself, and several turnoffs to points of interest.

Jubilee Pass–Salsberry Pass: Not heavily traveled but excellent route from Baker and points south, allowing a scenic and interest-packed drive up the floor of Death Valley past Badwater.

GRADED ROADS

North End: Graded road from Big Pine across Last Chance Range and past Sand Springs, entering Death Valley near Ubehebe Crater: 76 miles without roadside development of any kind, a road only for the self-sufficient. Beautiful desolate flats dotted with dry bushes and flanked by wrinkled ranges and peaks. Road is easily passable, but is subject to washouts in summer and is not regularly patrolled. Inquire about current conditions, and check in and out with responsible authorities.

Titus Canyon: Outstanding mountain and canyon entrance from Beatty. See chapter on back country trips for details; road closed in summer.

Greenwater Valley: Route connects from near Shoshone to near Dante's View. Sweeping, open country with several side roads, most of them little traveled and seldom patrolled.

Saratoga Springs: Road follows along the Amargosa River, entering Death Valley from the southeast with the entire valley spreading ahead. Road often is rough, may be closed in summer and is not patrolled daily.

PUBLIC TRANSPORTATION

Service varies from year to year; for latest information consult the National Park Service or any of the hostelries. Train and bus travelers may stop over in Las Vegas and rent a car, or may take the Las Vegas–Tonopah–Reno Stage Line, which schedules regular trips into Death Valley in season. Conducted motor tours from Las Vegas and Los Angeles are operated by Riddle Scenic Tours (206 West 6th Street, Los Angeles, California 90014) and Tanner-Gray Line Motor Tours (1207 West 3rd Street, Los Angeles, California 90017).

AIRPORTS

Paved 3,070-foot landing strip and tie-down at Furnace Creek Village. Gravel 1,600-foot strip and tie-down at Stove Pipe Wells Hotel. Aviation gasoline at Furnace Creek. Lights only at Furnace Creek field, by request. No scheduled air transportation; charter bush flights from Lone Pine and Las Vegas.

LODGING

The main season is from late October to early April, with advance reservations advisable, especially for holidays. Some hostelries are open the year around; remember that temperatures are cooler at the higher elevations. All lodging facilities in Death Valley are privately owned and operated except for Wild Rose Station, which is franchised by the National Park Service.

INSIDE THE MONUMENT

Furnace Creek Inn: Luxury hotel with striking architecture and palm gardens; American plan. Dining room, cocktail lounge, gift shop, barber and beauty shops, laundry service, garage. Tennis courts and warm-water swimming pool on the grounds; golf course at nearby Furnace Creek Ranch. Open from early November to Easter; accommodates 135 guests. Elevation, sea level.

Address: Fred Harvey Hotels, 530 West 6th Street, Los Angeles, California 90014.

Furnace Creek Ranch: Accommodations range from sleeping cabins without bath to four-room housekeeping cottages. Cafeteria, fountain, grocery store, gift

FURNACE CREEK INN

shop. Commercial date orchard on the grounds; also a museum (free) and outdoor displays of early-day mining equipment and wagons. Swimming pool; nine-hole golf course; saddle horses. Check for current schedule of activities and entertainment such as rides, dances, movies. Open from mid-October through April; accommodates 400 guests. Elevation −178 feet.

Address: Fred Harvey Hotels, 530 West 6th Street, Los Angeles, California 90014.

Stove Pipe Wells Hotel: Hotel rooms opening onto patio and lobby; cottages with and without bath. Dining room, fountain, bar, gift shop, swimming pool. Evening slide programs twice weekly and patio dancing. Open all year; accommodates 286 guests. Elevation, sea level.

Address: Stove Pipe Wells Hotel, Death Valley, California.

Wild Rose Station: Cabins with bath; coffee shop and gift shop. Open the year around; accommodations for 10 guests. Elevation 3,500 feet.

Address: Wild Rose Station Resort, Trona, California.

NEAR THE MONUMENT

Beatty: East of Death Valley, in Nevada; established concurrently with Rhyolite. Motels, hotels, cafes, cocktail lounges, gambling houses, general store, post office. Elevation, 3,400 feet.

Shoshone: East of Death Valley on the route from Baker; a travelers' oasis and supply center dating from the turn-of-the-century mine boom. Motel, cafe, cocktail lounge, grocery, post office. Community swimming pool is open to overnight guests. Elevation 3,400 feet.

Trona: West of Death Valley in Panamint Valley; grown up around chemical plants that are processing the dry bed of Searles Lake. Motels, cafes, cocktail lounges, grocery and general stores, post office. Trona is the largest of the towns on the edge of Death Valley, with the most complete range of goods and services. Elevation 1,600 feet.

CAMPGROUNDS

Public campgrounds and small secondary camp sites with little development are maintained by the National Park Service. Check at the Visitor Center or ranger stations for detailed information. Water is available unless otherwise noted, but should be purified before drinking except at Furnace Creek, Texas Spring, Mesquite Spring, and Emigrant Junction. Firewood must not be cut from mesquite trees, nor may bushes be broken or uprooted; desert vegetation is too slow growing to provide wood for the fires of great numbers of campers. Camp stoves are an ideal solution, or firewood may be purchased at Furnace Creek Ranch or Stove Pipe Wells Hotel. Most campgrounds are open the year around, but those at sea level or below are not recommended for summer use because of the heat. During the main season, November through April, stays are limited to 30 days in the main campgrounds. No advance reservations can be accepted. Gusty winds make it advisable to anchor tents well, and to lower them to the ground when leaving camp for the day.

CENTRAL VALLEY

Furnace Creek: Adjacent to the Visitor Center. Mesquite and athel trees offer some privacy and shade; area quickly becomes dusty when use is heavy. Ten developed sites plus overflow space; flush toilets. Elevation −190 feet.

Sand Dunes: Near Stove Pipe Wells Hotel, on the edge of the Dunes. Twenty-five undeveloped sites; pit toilets; no water. Elevation, below sea level. Closed in summer.

Texas Spring: Nestled among bare clay hills near Furnace Creek; open gravel slope. Eighty-five sites; flush toilets. Elevation, sea level. Closed in summer.

NORTH VALLEY

Midway Well: Off the Scotty's Castle road at the edge of low mesquite-covered sand dunes. Ten undeveloped sites; pit toilets. Elevation, sea level. Closed in summer.

Mesquite spring: In a grove of large mesquite growing at a continuously flowing spring; partially shaded. Thirty sites; pit toilets. Elevation 1,800 feet (likely to be cold in winter).

SOUTH VALLEY

Bennett's Well: At the base of the Panamint Mountains on the west side of the Valley; no trees. Five sites; no toilets. Elevation, below sea level.

TEXAS SPRING CAMPGROUND

FUNERAL MOUNTAINS

Daylight Pass: Open saddle with a few willows, near east boundary of the Monument on the Beatty road. Six undeveloped sites; pit toilets. Elevation 4,300 feet.

PANAMINT MOUNTAINS

Emigrant Junction: Adjacent to the ranger station, in a grove of athel trees. Three sites; flush toilets nearby. Elevation 2,160 feet.

Mahogany Flat: Sweeping overlook of Death Valley from the head of Wildrose Canyon; pine trees. Road is unpaved and steep, not suitable for trailers; often blocked by snow in winter. Eight sites, pit toilets, no water. Elevation 8,200 feet (fine for summer camping; snowed-in most winters).

Thorndike: Among the pinyon pines and junipers of upper Wildrose Canyon. Ten sites, pit toilets, water usually frozen in winter and road often snowed-in. Elevation 7,500 feet.

Wildrose: A clearing beneath trees near Wildrose Ranger Station. Eight sites; pit toilets. Elevation 4,100 feet.

PICNIC AREAS

All campgrounds and camp sites may be used for picnicking; also springs and widened spots along road shoulders.

TRAILERS

A shaded trailer court with water and power connections, showers, toilets, and laundry facilities is operated at Furnace Creek Ranch by Fred Harvey Company. Facilities are also available in communities near the Monument such as Beatty, Shoshone, and Trona. Trailers are permitted in Texas Spring Campground and at the secondary camp sites, but there are no hook-ups. Holding tank disposal stations for trailers are at Furnace Creek and Mesquite Spring campground.

FACILITIES AND SERVICES

Facilities and services within the Monument and near its borders change from year to year; check with the National Park Service for up-to-date information.

Gasoline and Oil (year around): Furnace Creek Village, Shoshone, Beatty, Scotty's Castle, Slim's Place (on U.S. 95 at the head of Grapevine Canyon road), Stove Pipe Wells Hotel, Panamint Springs Resort, Wild Rose Station, Trona.

Meals and Snacks: Furnace Creek Ranch (in season only), Furnace Creek Inn (in season only, and by advance reservation only except for guests), Shoshone, Beatty, Scotty's Castle, Stove Pipe Wells Hotel (snacks only during the summer), Panamint Springs Resort, Wild Rose Station, Trona.

Groceries: Furnace Creek Ranch (in season only), Stove Pipe Wells Hotel (small selection of basic items only), Shoshone, Beatty, Trona.

Showers: Furnace Creek Village.

Self-Service Laundry: Furnace Creek Village.

Post Office: Outgoing mail may be left at any hostelry. Post offices are at Furnace Creek Village, Beatty, Shoshone, and Trona.

Telephone: National Park Service Visitor Center, Furnace Creek Village, Furnace Creek Inn, Stove Pipe Wells Village, and Emigrant Ranger Station. In emergencies, park rangers can handle messages by radio.

Automobile Repairs and Towing Service: Furnace Creek Inn (in season), Beatty, Shoshone, Trona.

Medical Service: An infirmary usually is operated at Furnace Creek Inn, in season. Lone Pine and Trona have modern hospitals. Check with the National Park Service for current information, or in case of emergency.

Information: Park Service Visitor Center, any ranger station, any hostelry.

PROGRAMS AND RECREATION

Talks: Brief slide program given hourly at the Visitor Center (no charge); also illustrated talks by park naturalists each evening throughout the season (ask

NATIONAL PARK VISITOR CENTER

about current schedule). Naturalist programs two nights or more per week, in season, at Stove Pipe Wells Hotel. Occasional campfire programs as demand warrants.

Nature Walks and Auto Caravans: Schedule varies from year to year; check at the Visitor Center or any ranger station.

Museums: National Park Service Visitor Center and Furnace Creek Village.

Movies: Occasionally at Furnace Creek Village; check for current information.

Dances: Occasionally at Furnace Creek Village and Stove Pipe Wells Hotel; check for current information.

Church Services: Both Catholic and Protestant, during the season, in the Furnace Creek area; ask about current arrangements. Special Easter sunrise service most years.

'49ers Encampment: Long weekend of special displays, contests, and programs held each November. Open to the public; ask for current year's dates and plans.

Swimming Pools (public): Furnace Creek Village, Stove Pipe Wells Hotel.

Saddle Horses: Furnace Creek Ranch.

NATIONAL PARK SERVICE

Death Valley was set aside as a National Monument in 1933, part of the National Park system of areas that are preserved for their scenic, scientific, and historic value: a part of the national heritage to be cared for and enjoyed by present generations, and passed on intact to future generations. To accomplish this, regulations stipulate that no animals shall be molested, plants removed or damaged, rocks collected, or historic or archeological sites disturbed. Park Service headquarters are in the Visitor Center at Furnace Creek. Rangers and naturalists are available the year around to answer questions and give assistance.

DESERT DRIVING SUGGESTIONS

Gas stations are far apart. Watch gas gauge, know how far to the next station.

Carry an accurate map. Know both present location and what lies ahead.

Grades are often much steeper than they look. This is especially true on alluvial fans. Use low gears going up hill to avoid engine "lug," and going downhill to avoid burning out brakes.

If the car boils, face it into the wind and leave the engine running at a fast idle. Sprinkle water over the radiator to speed cooling, but do not open the cap until the gauge shows that the water has cooled.

Vapor lock often causes trouble, especially when trying to start again after a long, hot drive. To clear it, cool the fuel pump by wrapping a wet cloth around it and waiting several minutes.

Conditions on back country roads change from time to time. Ask about the current situation before starting out. Let a responsible person (preferably a park ranger) know your plans, and check back in with the same person on return, or with someone who will notify him.

In remote country park on a slope, in order to coast if car fails to start readily.

Check on grades before plunging down; some are difficult to get back up.

HELL'S GATE

To prevent high-centering, drive with one set of wheels on the high center and the other along the edge of the road.

If stuck in sand don't spin the wheels; it will only dig the car in farther. If tires have tubes, let them down to about fifteen pounds and accelerate slowly and evenly; be sure to pump them up again when back on the highway. Tubeless tires tend to come off when let down low.

On narrow roads the right of way belongs to the ascending car.

A spare tire, jack, pump, tire irons, and repair kit are essentials for a back country trip. Two cars traveling together provide a margin of safety.

If trouble develops stay with the car. Park rangers can spot a car from the ground or the air much more easily than a person. In summer, get under the car for shade. Hub caps can be used for shovels. Radiator water can be used to make wet compresses, or to drink if it has no additives. Mirrors can be used for signaling. Tires can be burned to make black smoke for a distress signal.

HOT WEATHER PRECAUTIONS

Carry water for both passengers and car. One gallon per person per day and five gallons for the radiator are minimum allowances in hot weather. Carry more if going into the back country.

Stay on main roads, the only ones fully maintained and patrolled in summer: California State Highway 190, the Emigrant Pass and Wildrose Canyon road in the Panamints, the Daylight Pass road to Beatty, and Scotty's Castle road.

Maintain proper tire pressure on the highway. Heat generated by soft tires may cause blowouts.

Avoid overexposure to the sun. Sunburn, heat stroke, or heat exhaustion can be serious. Wear shirt and hat while in the sun.

If walking is necessary because of emergency, do so only during the coolest part of the night (from 10 P.M. to sunup) and stay in the shade during daylight hours. Carry as much water as possible, and drink it rather than conserving it. At least one gallon will be needed for each twenty miles of summer nighttime walking. Walk along a road if possible and every few miles arrange stones or brush saying "Help," with an arrow pointing in the direction of travel. However, do not walk if stranded in a car; *stay with the car* until help comes.

Reading List

ADAMS, ANSEL, NANCY NEWHALL, and RUTH KIRK. *Death Valley*. San Francisco: Five Associates, 1954. Striking photographs, plus narrative and quick guide.

AMERICAN GUIDE SERIES. *Death Valley*. Boston: Houghton, Mifflin, 1939. Outdated as a guide but valuable for historical information.

CHALFANT, W. A. *Death Valley, the Facts*. Stanford: Stanford University Press, 3rd ed., 1936. Standard factual summation; slightly outdated.

COOLIDGE, DANE. *Death Valley Prospectors*. New York: E. P. Dutton & Co., 1937. Anecdotal account from the forty-niners to Death Valley Scotty.

DRISKILL, EARL C. *Death Valley Scotty Rides Again*. Death Valley: Earl C. Driskill, 1955. Scotty's tales of the glory days.

FERRIS, ROXANA S., drawings by JEANNE R. JANISH. *Death Valley Wildflowers*. Death Valley: Death Valley Natural History Association, 1962. Drawings and descriptions of the most common flowers, ferns, cacti, bushes and trees.

GLASSCOCK, C. B. *Here's Death Valley*. New York: Bobbs Merrill, 1940. The mining heyday, with stories based on interviews of old timers who lived them.

JAEGER, EDMUND C. *Desert Wildflowers*. Stanford: Stanford University Press, rev. ed. 1964. Accepted standard field identification book.

JAEGER, EDMUND C. *Desert Wildlife*. Stanford: Stanford University Press, 1961. Describes common mammals, birds, reptiles, insects, and mollusks.

LEE, BOURKE. *Death Valley Men*. New York: Macmillan, 1932. The men who lived in Death Valley during the rollicking opening decades of the century.

MANLY, WILLIAM LEWIS. *Death Valley in '49*. Los Angeles: Borden Publishing Company, 1949. Manly's own account of the forty-niners' sad trek, written several years afterward.

MAXON, JOHN H. *Death Valley: Origin and Scenery*. Death Valley: Death Valley Natural History Association, 1963. Geology summary; non-technical.

PUTNAM, GEORGE PALMER. *Death Valley and Its Country*. New York: Duell, Sloan & Pearce, 1946. Description of the valley and tales of the early days.

PUTNAM, GEORGE PALMER. *Death Valley Handbook*. New York: Duell, Sloan & Pearce, 1947. Statistical summary of natural history and history.

WELLES, RALPH E. and FLORENCE B. *The Bighorn of Death Valley*. Washington, D.C.: Government Printing Office, 1961. Detailed study of bighorn sheep.

WILSON, NEIL C. *Silver Stampede*. New York: Macmillan, 1937. The story of Panamint City, Death Valley's first boom camp.

Index

Page references in italics refer to illustrations.

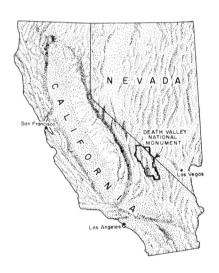